番を待つ2つのお弁当

'FOR BREAKFAST
I EAT CONVENIENCE STORE BREAD,
FOR LUNCH I EAT CONVENIENCE STORE RICE BALLS
WITH SOMETHING FROM THE HOT FOOD CABINET,
AND AFTER WORK I'M OFTEN SO TIRED
I JUST BUY SOMETHING FROM THE STORE
AND TAKE IT HOME FOR DINNER.

WHEN I THINK THAT MY BODY
IS ENTIRELY MADE UP OF FOOD FROM THIS STORE,
I FEEL LIKE I'M AS MUCH A PART OF THE STORE
AS THE MAGAZINE RACKS OR THE COFFEE MACHINE.'

**SAYAKA MURATA,
*CONVENIENCE STORE WOMAN***

TIM ANDERSON

簡単日本食

BOWLS & BENTO

JAPANEASY

SIMPLE AND SATISFYING JAPANESE RECIPES
FOR ALL DAY, EVERY DAY

Hardie Grant

BOOKS

1

**RICE
PICKLES
SOUP**

22

2

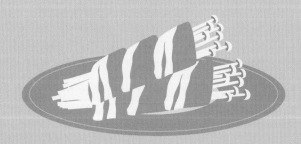

SMALL SIDES

86

3

BIG SIDES
RICE BOWL TOPPINGS
ONE-DISH DINNERS

138

4

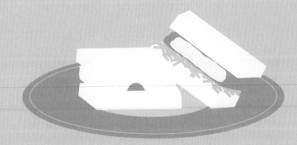

BREAD & PASTRIES

178

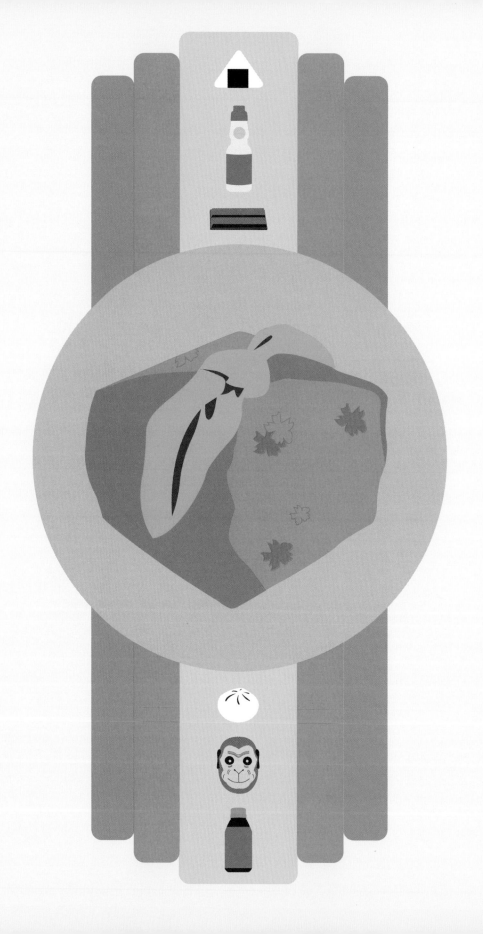

PREFACE

I wanted to call this book *Your Home Conbini,* but my publishers were like, 'Hmm, no, we let you do *Your Home Izakaya* and we're not super stoked about doing another book with a word in its title that not everybody understands.' Fair enough. So, then I proposed *Bento, Breakfasts and Bowls*, which has a nice rhythm to it, with the same jaunty cadence as Guy Fieri's seminal *Diners, Drive-ins and Dives*, and I do love a little alliteration. Besides, *Bento, Breakfasts and Bowls* tells you exactly what you're getting! But after some discussion, my editor cut 'Breakfasts' in the name of brevity and marketability. How dare her! It's the most important meal of the day!!!

But let me explain why I wanted conbini as part of the title in the first place. For the uninitiated, conbini (or, if we want to be pedantic about romanisation, *konbini*) are Japanese convenience stores and, although they're a very mundane part of life in Japan, they're also truly magical places. This may sound absurd, but sometimes when I'm really missing Japan, I listen to conbini in-store advertising jingles and door-chime music on YouTube and have a little cry. All right, I don't actually cry, but these cheery melodies were once part of the soundtrack to my life and hearing them does momentarily bring me back to a happy place.

It's not just rose-tinted old-man wistfulness that makes me miss conbini; they really are objectively wonderful. The food at conbini is always fresh, varied, nourishing and even exciting. You can grab a classic bento, ramen salad, or egg sandwich, or you can take your time and seek out something new – a limited-edition KitKat bar, a seasonal steamed bun, or even a regional speciality that may not be sold at branches of the same shop in other parts of the country. Conbini are remarkable – a real triumph of logistics, food manufacturing and good old-fashioned capitalism.

Nowadays, my emotional connection to Japanese food is a mix of nostalgia for things I've had before, comfort from the things I eat routinely and excitement for the things I haven't tried yet, or don't get to have very often. Japanese convenience stores tick all three of those boxes, not to mention flavour, balance and satisfaction. And they do it quickly and consistently, twenty-four hours a day. You can always, always count on conbini.

Another thing I always miss about Japan are traditional Japanese breakfasts. To be honest, I eat these much more as a returning visitor to Japan than I did as a resident there. My breakfast was usually an onigiri (rice ball) or two and a bottle of tea from (surprise surprise) the conbini. Japanese breakfasts are highly varied and they feel nourishing and complete in a way that Western breakfasts rarely do. They are based on the super-satisfying power couple of rice and miso soup, accompanied by a variety of small vegetable and protein side dishes, such as grilled fish, eggs, pickles, nori, nattō, maybe even a little salad. The permutations are endless, and that's part of the appeal – they never get boring because there are always little variations you can make to change them up.

I don't recall exactly what prompted this – my therapist would probably tell you it's something to do with my control issues and a need to create order out of chaos – but last year, I decided to try to make Japanese breakfasts as often as I could. Maybe not every day, but most days. This was facilitated by having more time at home, a change that was partly necessitated by the pandemic and partly a conscious decision. (It was also made possible by my purchase of a fancy rice cooker, which I will get into later.) But more than that, having Japanese breakfasts on a near-daily basis was made possible by maintaining a simple modus operandi: *make my refrigerator into my own little conbini*, always full of pre-prepared food (and drinks) from which I can cobble together a delicious Japanese meal in a matter of minutes. In Japanese, this practice is called *tsukurioki* – roughly, 'make ahead' – and it is key to having good food at the ready, 24/7.

This is a book of recipes, of course, but it's also a sort of strategy guide. Most of the recipes in this book can be prepped ahead and eaten later, either cold or reheated. In fact, some of the recipes actually improve after a day or two in the refrigerator. And the few things that can't be made ahead are super quick. This will allow you to have Japanese food for breakfast, lunch and dinner in a matter of minutes – honestly, with a little planning and the right kit, you can have a Japanese meal in the amount of time it takes to boil the kettle and make a cup of tea.

The whole conbini ethos is that everybody deserves a good meal, at any time of day, every day of the week and I hope to show you how you can provide that same service for yourself or your family at home. This is everyday self-care and self-love, in rice bowl, lunchbox and breakfast form. Because after all, Japanese food is not just for special occasions – **Japanese food is forever**.

JAPANESE MEALS

EASY AS

(RICE) (PICKLES) (MISO SOUP)

There are many, many different ways to serve a Japanese meal. In *JapanEasy*, I think I rather glibly described the main styles of Japanese serving as 'one big thing, a bunch of little things or one big thing with a bunch of little things around it.' While this is not inaccurate, it is pretty flippant, and doesn't quite express the balance and variety found in traditional Japanese meals. In her book *Atsuko's Japanese Kitchen*, Atsuko Ikeda has a much more eloquent description of a typical Japanese dining structure, which she calls a 'triangle way' of eating: rice, pickles and soup provide the base of the triangle, with a large main dish at the top. (Side dishes may also be included, but they are optional.)

ONE SOUP, THREE SIDES (GIVE OR TAKE)

I particularly like Atsuko's explanation because it uses rice, pickles and soup as the foundation, just as in the traditional format known as *ichijū sansai* ('one soup, three sides'), but with greater flexibility that more accurately reflects how people in Japan actually eat. In ichijū sansai, rice and pickles are a given (they don't count as the 'three sides'), which means if you want to follow this structure to the letter, you're going to have a lot of prep to do. Luckily, you don't have to follow it to the letter. I recently discovered the Instagram hashtags for *ichijū nisai* (one soup, two sides), *ichijū issai* (one soup, one side), *ichijū yonsai* (four sides), etc., which serve to illustrate how real-life Japanese meals actually allow for quite a lot of freedom and variation.

But rice, pickles and soup are a great place to start when making a Japanese meal. This combination is satisfying, delicious, and perhaps, most importantly (because I'm a lazy git), easy – especially if you use pre-made or shop-bought pickles and soup. But rice is the most important part. I read somewhere a long time ago that Japanese food has no 'centre' – unlike traditional European meals, there is no 'main course,' and no particular emphasis on any one thing. If you were to describe Japanese food as 'meat and two veg', the two veg are just as important as the meat. So instead of a centre, they say Japanese food has a destination – and that destination is **rice**.

WELCOME TO RICE TOWN
POPULATION: YOU

Rice is the great satisfier – in many situations, a Japanese meal is just not complete without it. But, of course, a Japanese meal is not complete without other things, too – things to serve with rice, to mix into rice, to put on top of rice, and of course, things that are not rice at all and have nothing to do with rice! That's where this book comes in.

All of the recipes in this book fall into one (or more) of eight categories. The first three are:

(RICE)

(PICKLES)

(SOUP)

These provide the foundation on which to build innumerable Japanese meals. You won't need all of them all the time, but they're a great place to start. Add just one other thing, and you'll have a pretty satisfying meal. Which brings us to the next three categories:

(SMALL SIDES)

(BIG SIDES)

(RICE BOWL TOPPINGS)

Dishes in these categories are meant to be had alongside rice or on top of it, whether in a bento, a bowl or as part of a balanced breakfast. They can be veg, protein or a mix of both.

Mix and match them with a rice dish (plus pickles and soup, if you like) to create a wide variety of meals that can range from light lunches to big breakfasts to comforting donburi dinners. For example:

A   +   B   +   C   +   D

will provide a simple but satisfying
breakfast, lunch or light dinner

A   +   B   +   D   +   D

will make a lovely bento

A   +   B   +   C

(in a flask)

+

D   +   D

will make an even lovelier bento

Or you can strip it back, and just make one big thing to have with rice:

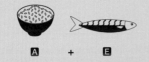

A   +   E

for a super-simple bento or dinner

A   +   F

for a hearty rice bowl

And of course you can always add some **B** or a **C** to these if you're feeling it. Not so into carbs? You can make a meal of **B**, **C** and a couple of **D**s. In the mathematics of Japanese food, there are no wrong answers! Mix and match as you like... or don't! You can also just have one thing, which brings us to:

(ONE-DISH DINNERS)

These are big bowls and plates that satisfy all on their own, incorporating rice and noodles – no need for sides. Some of them overlap with **E** and **F**, or even **A**, in the case of one-pot mixed rice dishes. These are hearty, filling dishes like ramen and donburi that can be made from pre-prepared toppings – or from scratch – very quickly. Finally, it's just not a conbini, at home or otherwise, without baked goods! The humble sandwich is just as much a staple of Japanese lunches as rice balls or bento. So I've included a final category:

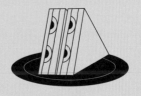

(BREAD AND PASTRIES)

This is where you'll find iconic items like the classic katsu sando, as well as other lesser-known delights like hot dog rolls and a few sweets. These are sometimes substantial enough to be a meal on their own, but they can be served with other things, as well. The bread and filling in any given sandwich kind of occupy the 'rice and side dish' part of a meal, so add a soup and some pickles and you should have a very satisfying lunch.

Each recipe includes a serving temperature as well as a shelf life, so you'll have an idea of how they'll work in a bento or other pre-prepared meal. So there you have it: easy Japanese bento and bowls (and breakfasts and breads) which you can make by mixing and matching any of these recipes however you like. Not sure where to start? Take a look at the following pages for few meal plan ideas.

A CLASSIC, HEALTHY
JAPANESE BREAKFAST

A Sweet Potato, Chestnut and Millet Rice (page 31)
B Yuzu-pickled Fennel (page 55)
C Homemade Instant Miso Soup (page 75)
D Salted Salmon (page 124)
D Three Ways with Nattō (pages 58–61)

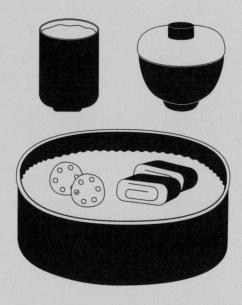

AN EVEN SIMPLER BUT
JUST AS FILLING BENTO

A Classic Root Vegetable Rice (page 34)
D Japanese Omelette, Three Ways (pages 96–97)

A SIMPLE BUT
FILLING BENTO

A Classic Root Vegetable Rice (page 34)
D Kinpira Beetroot (page 116)
D Mackerel Simmered with Onions
and Ginger (page 128)

A FULL 'ICHIJŪ SANSAI' FEAST FOR DINNER
OR LUNCH, TO MAKE IN 30 MINUTES
(GIVE OR TAKE) WHILE THE RICE COOKS:

A Green Pea Rice (page 36)
B Smoky Pickled Daikon (page 63)
C Shimeji Mushroom and Okra Miso Soup (page 80)
D Microwaved Pea Shoots with Gomashio (page 106)
D Enoki Bacon Rolls (page 102)
D Spicy Avocado and Tofu Salad (page 119)

A MINIMUM EFFORT, MAXIMUM 'WOW FACTOR' DINNER:

A Sea Bream Rice (page 45)
B Salted Chinese Leaf with Sanshō (page 69)
C Clam Miso Soup (page 36)
D Microwaved Asparagus and Spring Onions with Mustard Miso Vinegar Sauce (page 110)

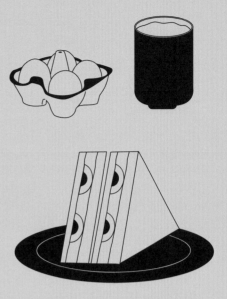

SOMETHING FOR WHEN YOU REALLY, REALLY WANT EGGS

H Egg Sandwich, Three Ways (pages 193–194)

SOMETHING TO SHOVEL INTO YOUR MOUTH WHILE BINGE WATCHING… OH, LET'S SAY *BOJACK HORSEMAN*, BECAUSE I THINK MORE PEOPLE SHOULD WATCH *BOJACK HORSEMAN*. (IT'S REALLY GOOD!)

G Spaghetti Napolitan (page 158)
F Gyoza-filling Rice Bowl (page 144)
G Cheesy Yakisoba Omelette (page 174)

AND FINALLY, SOMETHING FOR DESSERT

H Sweet Red Bean Buns (page 186)

So you see, there's a Japanese meal to suit every occasion, every mood and every schedule! Just remember: everything is easier if you make it easier, and the next section will provide some tips on exactly how to do this.

YOUR HOME
CONBINI
KITCHEN

USEFUL EQUIPMENT

If you've read my previous books, particularly the others in the *JapanEasy* series, you've probably heard me say that you don't need any specialist equipment to cook Japanese food. Well, I lied. Sort of. It's true that you don't need any specialist equipment, but there are three things that will make cooking Japanese food much quicker, easier and more pleasurable, which means you will be doing it more regularly. They are:

A MICROWAVE,

A GOOD RICE COOKER

AND THE RIGHT CROCKERY.

1
THE MICROWAVE

Most of you probably already have a microwave, so let's talk about that one first. For a long time, I didn't have a microwave. I didn't really think I was missing anything – what are they good for, anyway, other than reheating lasagne? But now I don't know how I lived without my microwave. Of course, it's good for reheating stuff, which is particularly useful if you plan to stock your refrigerator with pre-prepared dishes, like I do. But it turns out it's actually an amazing cooking device, too.

Microwave cooking seems to get a bad rap in this country, like it's somehow a cheat or produces inferior results. And that is true of some things (please don't cook steak in the microwave), but in general, it produces remarkably delicious food, very efficiently – especially vegetables. I follow a lot of Japanese easy recipe accounts on Instagram (which are listed in Resources, page 210) and most of them cook veg, and many other things, in the microwave as a matter of routine. These accounts are what prompted me to start experimenting with microwave cooking myself and, let me tell you, it is honestly now my preferred cooking method for most vegetables.

Microwaves cook by agitating the water molecules within the food itself, so this essentially causes veg to steam from the inside out. This makes for beautifully cooked veg, with no loss in colour or flavour and, because the cooking is instantaneous, it can be fine-tuned down to the second. And it's just so fast. If you want to hit your five-a-day, or your three sides to have in a 'one soup, three sides' meal, then the microwave is your best friend. Simply whack some veg in a microwaveable container, cover it loosely, zap it for a couple minutes and dress it with amenable Japanese seasonings – there are specific recipes starting on page 106.

But if the microwave is your best friend, a good rice cooker is your soul mate – supportive, reliable, helping you to be your best self. I had a rice cooker in college and when I lived in Japan, but then, for years, I didn't have one. I thought I didn't need it, and I was proud of my hard-earned stovetop rice cooking method, which took me years to perfect. But when I decided to start eating Japanese breakfasts every day, I figured getting a good rice cooker would make the task far more achievable. What do I mean by 'good' rice cooker? I mean it should have multiple functions and computerised cooking technology; one that doesn't have these really isn't any better than a saucepan, so don't bother. My rice cooker has settings for slow-cooking, steaming, porridge, brown rice, scorched rice and incubating yogurt, among other things, but the key advantages are that it has a delayed start timer and it makes really good rice – annoyingly, much better than rice I cook on the hob. And it does it effortlessly.

It is no exaggeration to say my rice cooker has been life-changing. It has single-handedly allowed me to have Japanese meals on a more regular basis – especially breakfast. I am not a morning person. I hate getting out of bed. But let me tell you, when I smell that rice wafting up from downstairs in the morning, I don't even care what time it is – I'm getting up. Fresh rice from the cooker makes mornings a joy rather than a struggle.

Equally, having the right crockery makes eating Japanese meals more enjoyable and actually more achievable. I've always said you can have Japanese food served on any old dishes you have and that is true – if you're having one soup, three sides, it's okay if the three sides are all on one big plate and the soup is in a novelty mug, preferably one that says something like 'I don't need Google, my wife knows everything!' or 'Definitely not vodka! ;)'. I do love a novelty mug, me. But Japanese food looks better and is easier to serve if you have a wide variety of plates, bowls and sauce pots to choose from. Rice bowls and miso soup bowls in particular are important and, for the latter, I'd always go for the kind with lids, which help keep the soup hot. It may go without saying that you will also need chopsticks and, if you can find them, chopstick rests (*hashi-oki*). These are strictly 'nerd-level' accessories, but they look classy and cute and they do help keep the table clean.

And then, of course, there are bento, which I discuss in more detail on pages 91–93. But very generally speaking, a good bento to get you going should be leakproof, microwaveable, freezable and offer some flexibility in terms of their interior space – so ones with removable dividers are ideal.

Apart from these three essentials – which are not essential at all, really – there are just a few other things you might want. I find my **rice-washing bowl**, which is basically a bowl with a sieve built into the side, very handy. A **Japanese-style grater** is also useful for making quick work of ginger, garlic, daikon, or other things that require a very thorough grating. Finally, a cast iron or non-stick **rectangular Japanese egg pan** is a must if you plan on making Japanese omelettes (pages 96–97) with any regularity. For garnishes, you may also want to invest in little **star-**, **heart-** or **flower-shaped vegetable cutters**, which are wholly unnecessary but are an easy way to add a bit of visual fun to your meals (see Bento Basics, page 91, for more on this).

That's about it. Oh, and you need a decent knife too. Make sure you have a knife! I talk to many home cooks who fall at the first hurdle when cooking Japanese food because they do not own a knife.

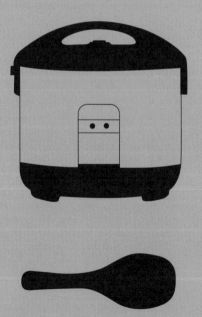

4
REFRIGERATOR AND PANTRY STAPLES

More information on ingredients can be found in the glossary (pages 208–209), but for now I just want to mention the few things you'll want to have on hand at all times: dashi powder, soy sauce, sake, mirin, rice vinegar, both red and white miso, Japanese rice, sesame oil and toasted sesame seeds. None of these need to be of particularly high quality, but they do all need to be Japanese – Chinese versions don't taste the same and European brands often just taste terrible.

One of the rules I have for myself as a cook is: don't make it if you can buy it. I don't mean this literally, of course. There's lots of stuff I make that I could potentially buy. What I really mean is: don't make it if you can buy it and it's of comparable quality and still affordable. This mantra will simply make your life easier; if Japanese meals are usually going to involve miso soup and pickles, it makes sense to have miso soup and pickles on hand – and these absolutely do not have to be homemade. There is some really good instant miso soup out there (Marukome is a decent, widely available brand) and the same goes for pickles. I'm not saying don't make your own miso soup and pickles, that would be self-defeating and idiotic in a book which contains eight soup recipes and nine pickle recipes. Just don't feel like you have to make them all the time!

5
DRINKS

Besides ingredients and store-bought shortcuts like those mentioned previously, one other thing you'll want to have to complete your home conbini setup is drinks. Again, these can be shop-bought and can include a wide variety of Japanese soft drinks, such as ramune (Japanese lemonade) or Yakult and Calpis, as well as not-so-soft drinks, i.e., canned shōchū highballs, sake and beer. But the Japanese drink I find most versatile, and the most worth making yourself, is iced tea. It's hard to get good iced tea in the UK that isn't jam-packed with sugar (Japanese iced tea is generally unsweetened) and, besides, buying bottled iced tea is a terrible waste of plastic. I simply buy Japanese tea – loose leaf or in teabags, it doesn't matter – and cold-infuse it in a big jug in the refrigerator so it's basically on tap whenever I need it. (Which is approximately every 40 minutes.) My favourite iced teas are genmaicha (toasted rice tea), hōjicha (roasted green tea) and mugicha (not an actual tea, but an infusion of dark-roasted barley grains). But drink whatever you like – cold, sweet, milky black teas (especially Royal Milk Tea, which was invented by Lipton Japan in 1965, but is now practically generic) are probably just as popular in Japan as more traditional green teas and their milk.

Of course, coffee is equally key to the conbini experience, but I find cold-brewing it is too much of a faff. Instead, I make a pot of filter coffee and then chill it down, which is more like what you'd get in Japan anyway. Whether you're drinking tea or coffee, simply decant them into water bottles as soon as they're cool enough, so you can grab one or two on the way out the door in the morning.

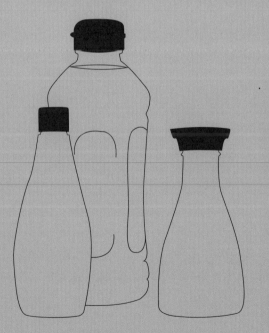

READ THESE NOTES
BEFORE COOKING

SORRY TO SHOUT, BUT THEY ARE IMPORTANT!

1

Recipe yields can vary widely depending on how many other dishes you are serving them with. (For example, a dish that serves two on its own may make enough for as many as eight bento, if the bento contains several other things.)

3

Most recipes can be scaled up or down reasonably well; I have indicated wherever there may be issues with this.

4

Sugar indicates white caster (superfine) or granulated sugar unless another kind is specified.

5

Oil indicates neutral vegetable oil.

6

Butter must be unsalted.

7

Use fresh ingredients unless frozen, dried or tinned are specified.

8

Vinegar indicates Japanese rice vinegar.

9

Use fine salt unless sea salt flakes are specified.

2

Serving temperatures are also provided for each recipe; although note that things that can be served at room temperature should still be kept refrigerated until ready to eat.

10

All seasoning is to taste, and quantities provided are suggestions; if you are sensitive to salt, consider reducing quantities of soy sauce, miso, salt, etc. You can always add more later.

11

Dashi indicates prepared liquid dashi; dashi powder indicates the powder itself.

12

Many sauce and marinade recipes are embedded within the dishes that use them, but they are extremely versatile and can be made separately and applied to other dishes. For example, the carrot-miso dressing (page 172) will work well on any salad, the okonomiyaki dip (page 132) is delicious with fried food and the miso mustard vinegar sauce (page 112) tastes great with pretty much anything.

13

Soy sauce must be Japanese soy sauce.

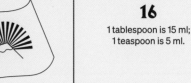

14

Rice must be Japanese short-grain rice.

15

Sesame oil and sesame seeds must always be toasted.

16

1 tablespoon is 15 ml; 1 teaspoon is 5 ml.

17

Measure by volume or weight as the recipe indicates.

18

Shelf lives are provided for each recipe, but they are approximate and refer to quality rather than safety. Don't throw obviously good food away just because I said it would only last a certain amount of time and, likewise, don't keep any food around if you suspect it's gone off. Use your best judgement and eyes and nose.

19

Miso can be any kind of miso unless a specific type is mentioned.

"I LIKE RICE. RICE IS GREAT WHEN YOU'RE HUNGRY AND YOU WANT TWO THOUSAND OF SOMETHING."

Mitch Hedberg

1

RICE

ご飯物

PICKLES

漬物

SOUP

汁物

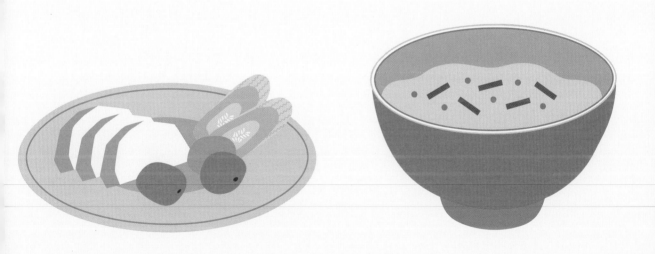

RICE

ご飯物

PICKLES

漬物

SOUP

汁物

These are the building blocks – the foundation of Japanese meals, the Holy Trinity of satisfaction. Some of the rice recipes and soups, in fact, can make filling meals all on their own. As for the pickles, it's always a good idea to have a few on the go in the refrigerator at all times, so they can lend their mouth-watering tang to liven up any meal.

RICE

A USER MANUAL

OKOME NO SETSUMEISHO お米の説明書

COOKING JAPANESE RICE IS SIMPLE – IT'S ALL ABOUT MEASUREMENTS AND TIMINGS.
HERE IS THE STOVETOP METHOD THAT HAS ALWAYS WORKED FOR ME:

1
MEASURE THE RICE

You will need 75 g (2½ oz) per portion, or 100 g (3½ oz) if you are a hungry rice monster. A 'rice cooker cup' (180 ml/6 fl oz/¾ cup, equivalent to one gō, a traditional Japanese unit of measure) holds 150 g (5 oz) of rice. All of the rice recipes in this book are based on this unit.

2
WASH THE RICE

This is primarily to remove excess starch. Wash the rice in three or four changes of water, swirling the grains gently each time. (If you're too rough with the rice, you can actually erode the grains and cause them to become even more starchy – so don't manhandle the rice!) Drain the rice well through a sieve with each wash.

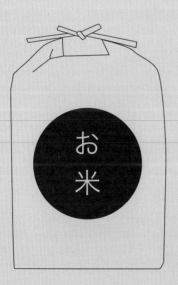

3
MEASURE THE WATER

I always do this by weight; it's more accurate. Specific quantities are given in each recipe, but the ratio for stovetop cooking is almost always 1 part rice to 1.3 parts water. So, for 4 portions/300 g/ 2 rice cooker cups of rice, you'll need 390 g (13¾ oz) of water. Rice cookers use different ratios, which change logarithmically with the amount of rice you're cooking. If you have a rice cooker, just make sure the liquid is at the correct indicated level for the amount of rice you're using, before you've added any additional solid ingredients (liquid seasonings such as mirin or soy sauce should be factored into the total volume).

4
COOK THE RICE

Again, if you have a rice cooker, just do what the rice cooker says. If you have a gas or electric hob,* place the rice and measured water in a saucepan with a snug-fitting lid, and place over a high heat, with the lid off. When the water boils, place a lid on the pan, and turn the heat all the way down. Set a timer for 15 minutes, and do not disturb the rice during this time. When the timer goes off, remove the lid and gently fluff the rice with chopsticks or a rice paddle, then put the lid back on the pan and leave to rest for another 10 minutes.

   *(If you have an induction hob: may God have mercy on your soul. Cooking rice on induction is fraught with peril. Follow the instructions above, but start the rice on low power; if you start high, the rice will stick to the bottom of the pan almost immediately, and your rice will be ruined. Proceed with caution!)

   Congratulations! You are now the proud parent of a healthy pan of plump, delicious Japanese rice. And there are so many exciting life paths it may embark upon! Your rice could even end up in a beautiful bento – which is certainly a thrill, but there are some things you should consider to best prepare your rice for this experience.

STORING AND REHEATING RICE

I am a naturalised British citizen. I had to pass a test just to exist here! But that doesn't mean I fully understand this country. There are lots of little things that still just don't make sense to me, like Ant and Dec or how weddings go on for 16 hours, or why so many people are freaked out about reheating rice. I've heard countless people say that cooked rice should never be reheated – it's even on some food labels. *This is absolute nonsense.* **Rice is perfectly fine when it's reheated!**

But I understand where this anxiety comes from; the real risk is in leftover rice that hasn't been chilled down properly, because when rice sits out for too long, it has ideal conditions for microbial growth – warm, moist and starchy. And the 'do not reheat' rule probably stems from the fact that one of these microbes, bacillus cereus, cannot killed by reheating, and it can cause serious illness. **So don't worry about reheating rice – that's not the problem. Worry about getting your rice chilled down as quickly as you can! The best way to do this is to put it on a plate or container in a shallow layer, and leave it uncovered until it cools to room temperature, then leave it in the refrigerator, still uncovered, until completely cold.** Once chilled, it will keep for up to five days, or it can be frozen. To freeze, it's best to wrap the rice up in individual portions so you can defrost just as much as you need, when you need it. Both refrigerated and frozen rice reheat beautifully in the microwave.

But if British conventional wisdom about leftover rice is far too cautious (and simply incorrect), then Japanese conventional wisdom can sometimes feel a bit too laissez-faire and inconsistent. In Japan, keeping rice at room temperature for several hours is standard practice and considered perfectly safe, but on the other hand, food shops, takeaways and convenience stores keep their cooked rice products such as onigiri and bento refrigerated at all times. What gives?

Well, there are some finer points to discuss here, not just with regards to safety but also flavour and texture. First of all, I am of the opinion that eating rice that's been sitting at room temperature for a few hours will still be safe to eat – so the typical Japanese practice of packing a bento with fresh rice in the morning, and eating it that day for lunch, will be fine. How have I come to this opinion? Well, because I've done it, hundreds of times. And not just me – it's the norm in Japan. And Japan cannot be said to have a rampant food poisoning problem.

Having said that, room temperature rice still makes me kinda nervous, and even in Japan it's considered best practice to refrigerate rice. The problem is that when you refrigerate rice, it deteriorates rapidly – it becomes dry and hard, with a dull, pasty flavour.

It's fine once it's reheated, but sometimes it's not meant to be reheated, as in onigiri or in bento made with a variety of cold items. But luckily, there are various workarounds and strategies to negotiate the quality-vs. -safety conundrum:

1

SEASON THE RICE

Salt and vinegar are preservatives, and using one or both of them to season your rice during or after cooking will make it less prone to spoilage at room temperature. Many of the rice recipes in this book already contain salt, and these will be absolutely fine if you make them in the morning and eat them at lunchtime. If you are having just plain rice, then mixing in a few spoonfuls of sushi vinegar (which you can buy at any Asian supermarket) when it's done cooking will work, too. As a bonus, vinegared rice tastes delicious, and if you do have to put it in the refrigerator later, it will be moister and more tender than unseasoned rice.

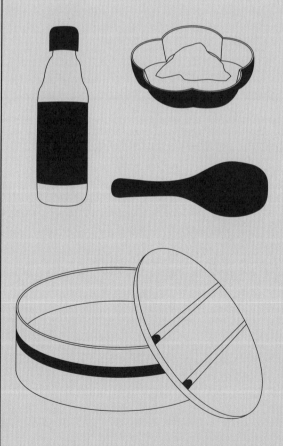

ご飯物 漬物 汁物

2

PRE-SOAK THE RICE
WITH BICARBONATE OF SODA

In Japan, rice destined for the refrigerator is usually cooked with enzymatic rice improvers that enhance and preserve its texture. These improvers are not that easy to get a hold of, and they're expensive, but you can achieve a similar result with good old bicarbonate of soda – a neat trick I discovered while writing *Tokyo Stories*, which has a chapter on conbini food. Basically, if you soak rice in a weak alkaline solution, it messes up the starches in the rice, so it stays soft even when completely chilled down in the refrigerator. Pretty cool! To do this, soak 300 g (10½ oz) of rice in 300 ml (10 fl oz/1¼ cups) water mixed with ¼ teaspoon bicarbonate of soda (baking soda) for 1½ hours, then drain and rinse the rice well, and proceed to cook it as usual. For rice that's going to be eaten cold, this really does work remarkably well, but it has some drawbacks: the cooked rice will have a slightly pale yellow colour and a faint 'bicarby' flavour, and it's not good warm – the texture is too soft.

3

FREEZE AND REHEAT THE RICE

Rice chilled down quickly and kept in the refrigerator will be safe to eat for about five days, but the sooner you eat it, the better. To maintain the texture and flavour of fresh rice longer, put it in the freezer as soon as you can after it's cooked, divided into individual portions and wrapped in cling film (plastic wrap). These can then simply be microwaved as needed, and this method has the additional benefit of the rice acting as a little ice pack, so it helps keep the rest of the food in your bento fresh, too. Of course, if you do this, you'll need a bento setup where the rice can be packed separately so it can be reheated on its own – more on this in the Bento Basics guide on page 92.

By the way, if you have a rice cooker with a 'keep warm' setting, these are designed to keep the rice hot enough to thwart microbial growth, so by all means, use it if you've got it. However, I must say I seldom use the keep warm function for more than a couple hours, because it rapidly dries out the rice, resulting in tough, chewy grains. But perhaps other rice cookers have better keep warm functionality – you'll have to try yours to see how the rice holds up.

EATING RICE

We've squared away how to cook, store and reheat rice, so here's the fun part: eating! And there are so many wonderful ways to eat rice. First of all, as lovely as rice is on its own, it likes company, and that can be something on the side, stirred through or on top – such as *furikake*, a dry seasoning to be sprinkled on top of rice that comes in hundreds of flavours. I am never without at least one packet of furikake at home; some of my favourites are yukari (shiso), *noritama* (nori and egg) and *chirimen sanshō* (baby sardine and Japanese pepper). These are invaluable for adding a bit of variety to meals.

The following recipes are all for variations on rice – some of them would be classified as *takikomi gohan* (rice cooked together with various ingredients), and some are called *mazegohan* (cooked rice with stuff mixed in at the end). When you first taste some of these, you may find they seem a little bit underseasoned – that's okay, because bear in mind they are generally meant to be eaten with more highly-seasoned side dishes or toppings. But if you're having a rice dish marked with **G** as a one-dish dinner on its own, you may want to add a bit of salt or soy sauce. Have fun with these, and try to match different types of rice to amenable sides – for example, the sesame, pickled ginger and nori rice (page 38) would be perfect with salmon, whereas the crab, sweetcorn and spring onion rice (page 48) would be excellent with a Japanese omelettes (pages 96–97) and a classic miso soup (page 75).

By the way, almost all of these recipes make fine onigiri – rice balls. You may struggle a bit shaping ones that have oily ingredients added, such as the 'un-fried' rice (page 41) or the smoked salmon and seaweed rice (page 42), but they'll still come together with a bit of extra pressure. If you're planning to make onigiri on a regular basis – and you should, because onigiri are delightful – then I would highly recommend investing in an onigiri mould. It just makes the process so much faster. I got one on eBay that makes six onigiri at once!

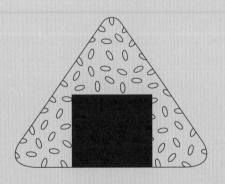

SWEET POTATO, CHESTNUT AND MILLET RICE

MOCHIKIBI IRI IMO-KURI GOHAN もちきび入り芋栗ご飯

SERVES 4

Sweet potatoes and chestnuts are often added to rice in Japan, adding a touch of earthy sweetness and – in the case of sweet potatoes – a pop of colour. On that note, use purple or white-fleshed sweet potatoes for this – orange ones become too soft when cooked. Millet is not common in either sweet potato rice or chestnut rice, but I include it here for a slightly nerdy reason, which is that it has been cultivated in Japan for at least as long as rice has been, but fell out of favour as a staple grain due to rice's socioeconomic and theocratic significance. So, I think millet deserves more love. It's already an important ingredient in certain Japanese dumplings and it's one of the primary staples in the indigenous Ainu cuisine – and besides, it tastes great, especially here, where its nutty flavour amplifies that of the potatoes and chestnuts.

Peel the potato or wash and scrub it very well, removing any stringy root fibres coming off it. Cut the potato and chestnuts into pieces about 1 cm (½ in) wide. Wash the rice and millet together, then combine in a rice cooker or saucepan along with the water, sake and salt. Proceed to cook using the same method for cooking white rice on page 27. When the rice is finished, carefully fold the potatoes and chestnuts through the rice. To serve, season each portion with a sprinkle of black sesame seeds and sea salt. Serve the rice hot or at room temperature. It lasts four days in the refrigerator or one month in the freezer.

150 g (5 oz) white or purple (not orange) sweet potato
100 g (3½ oz) cooked and peeled chestnuts
250 g (9 oz/⅙ cup) rice
50 g (2 oz) millet
400 g (14 oz) water
2 tablespoons sake
¼ teaspoon salt
black sesame seeds and sea salt, to taste

OAT, FREEKEH, BULGUR AND BLACK SESAME RICE

ŌTSU-MUGI, FURĪKA, BURUGURU TO KUROGOMA NO ZAKKOKUMAI

オーツ麦、フリーカ、ブルグルと黒ごまの雑穀米

SERVES 3–4

200 g (7 oz/scant 1 cup) rice
50 g (2 oz/¼ cup) cracked freekeh
30 g (1 oz/⅛ cup) cracked bulgur wheat
20 g (¾ oz/scant ¼ cup) rolled oats
    (don't use porridge oats or pinhead oats)
1 tablespoon black sesame seeds
400 g (14 oz) water

A little while ago, I had to have a word with myself about wholegrains. While I do like wholegrains, I don't *love* them like I love white rice or refined flour. But I'm a middle-aged man with high cholesterol who's overshot 'dad bod' and landed somewhere in the region of 'Santa bod', so I had to tell myself: 'Grow up. Get over it. Eat your wholegrains.' Yes, brown pasta isn't the nicest, but once it's covered in red sauce and Parmesan, does it really matter that much?

The answer, of course, is no, it's fine. But damn, sometimes you just can't beat plain white rice, and I do still have it with about half my Japanese meals. The rest of the time, I eat *zakkokumai*, a type of mixed rice that can contain any number of grains, seeds and pulses, but is still based on white rice. I would call this a compromise – except I really do love it too. I've experimented with various zakkokumai combos over the years and this is one of my favourites – the grains cook nicely together and have pleasantly nutty aromas that complement the rice without overpowering it.

Wash the rice and grains, drain well and combine with the sesame. Add the water and proceed to cook using the same method for cooking white rice on page 27. Serve the rice hot or at room temperature. It lasts four days in the refrigerator or one month in the freezer.

CLASSIC ROOT VEGETABLE RICE

TAKIKOMI GOHAN 炊き込みご飯

SERVES 3–4

2 small dried shiitake mushrooms
½ carrot (about 40 g/1½ oz peeled weight)
7.5 cm (3 in) chunk of burdock or
    Jerusalem artichoke (about 40 g/1½ oz)
2.5 cm (1 in) chunk of daikon (about
    40 g/1½ oz)
20 g (¾ oz) fried tofu (store-bought
    aburaage or tofu puffs work best)
2 tablespoons soy sauce (*usukuchi*, or
    light Japanese soy sauce, is preferable)
2 tablespoons sake
1 tablespoon mirin
300 g (10½ oz/2 rice cooker cups) rice
½ teaspoon dashi powder
¼ teaspoon salt
40–50 g (1½–2 oz) peas or *edamame* beans

My mother-in-law Emiko makes the best takikomi gohan. It is *so* good that my daughter rejects mine, brutally (but correctly) assessing it as inferior to her obāchan's. Frustrated with my failings, I asked Emiko for her recipe and she generously obliged – but mine *still* wasn't as good as hers when I made it her way. What was it? Was it her rice cooker? The kind of rice she buys? Was she deliberately sabotaging me, to curry favour with my daughter? Was she using higher-quality seasonings and fresh ingredients? All of the above? Most likely, she probably just doesn't follow her own recipe – she's more of a 'pinch of this, dash of that' kind of cook. The real secrets of world-class takikomi gohan may be forever locked within her brain. So, until we can download her consciousness onto a USB stick and plug it into a cooking robot, this recipe will have to do.

Place the mushrooms in a small bowl and cover with just-boiled water. Leave to steep and rehydrate for at least 20 minutes while you prepare the rest of the dish. Peel the root vegetables and cut them into matchsticks about 2.5 cm (1 in) long and no more than 5 mm (¼ in) wide. Cut the fried tofu into similar-sized pieces. Squeeze the mushrooms dry, but retain the liquid. Discard the mushroom stalks and cut the caps into pieces roughly the same size as the veg and tofu.

Combine the mushroom liquid with the other liquid seasonings and add enough fresh water to make 390 g (13¾ oz). Wash the rice and drain it well, then add it to the rice cooker or saucepan along with the seasoned water, dashi powder and salt. Briefly swirl the rice through the water to mix. Scatter the prepared veg and tofu over the surface of the rice and cook according to the instructions on page 27.

While the rice is cooking, warm the peas or beans in a microwave or by scalding with just-boiled water. When the rice is done, fold the peas or beans through with a spatula or rice paddle. Serve the rice hot or at room temperature. It lasts five days in the refrigerator or one month in the freezer.

GREEN PEA RICE

MAME GOHAN 豆ご飯

SERVES 3–4

300 g (10½ oz/2 rice cooker cups) rice
¼ teaspoon salt (optional)
big pinch of MSG (optional)
390 g (13¾ oz) water
100 g (3½ oz/⅔ cup) frozen peas

Here is a recipe so simple it feels silly to include it in a cookbook, but it's so versatile and useful, it would be a shame not to. All it is, really, is white rice with green peas; that's literally it. You hardly even need specific quantities. But it's one of the rice dishes I make the most, because I always have frozen peas on hand and because it goes with everything – seafood, meat, vegetables; traditional Japanese dishes or more modern recipes; spicy food, bland food; breakfast, lunch, dinner, whatever! And the pops of bright green against the white rice are like little emeralds. I love my *mame gohan*!

Cook the rice along with the seasonings, if using, with the measured water according to the instructions on page 27. While the rice is cooking, thaw the peas – you can do this in a microwave or simply by scalding with just-boiled water. When the rice is done, fold in the peas. That's it! Serve the rice hot or at room temperature. It lasts four days in the refrigerator or one month in the freezer.

CLAM MISO SOUP

ASARI NO MISOSHIRU あさりの味噌汁

SERVES 4

4 tablespoons sake
500 g (1 lb 2 oz) clams
600 ml (20 fl oz/2½ cups) dashi
handful of flat-leaf parsley leaves,
    pea shoots or other fresh, mild greens,
    roughly chopped
handful of chives, roughly chopped
60 g (2 oz) miso

This is one of my all-time favourite variations on miso soup, made with little clams. In Japan, they use a type of clam called *asari*, but any kind of small clam you can get will do, provided they are still in their shells. Whatever clams you use, ensure they are well cleaned and free of grit.

Combine the sake and clams in a saucepan, set over a high heat and bring to the boil. Place a lid on the pan and steam the clams for about 5 minutes, shaking the pan occasionally, until the clams have opened. Pour in the dashi and bring to a simmer. At this point, if there are any clams that haven't opened, fish them out and discard. Add the chopped greens, then remove from the heat and whisk in the miso and serve while still hot. This lasts five days in the refrigerator, but is best eaten immediately.

SESAME, PICKLED GINGER AND NORI RICE

BENI SHŌGA, IRIGOMA TO NORI NO MAZEGOHAN 紅生姜、炒りごまと海苔の混ぜご飯

SERVES 4

300 g (10½ oz/2 rice cooker cups) rice
2 tablespoons sesame seeds
½ teaspoon sugar
¼ teaspoon salt
¼ teaspoon sesame oil
390 g (13¾ oz) water
2 sheets of nori, crumpled and torn
    or snipped with scissors into flakes
40 g (1½ oz) red pickled ginger,
    finely chopped

The combination of toasted sesame seeds, pickled ginger and nori calls to mind the aromas of the *sushiya* (sushi restaurant), but it also features in several other Japanese dishes, such as yakisoba and ramen. There is a perfect completeness in this trio, like a major chord: the nori bringsa deep umami that underscores the nuttiness of the sesame, balanced and brightened by the sharp acidity of pickled ginger.

Wash the rice and combine in a rice cooker or saucepan along with the other ingredients, except the nori flakes and ginger. Cook everything according to the instructions on page 27. When the rice is done, fold in the nori and pickled ginger. Serve the rice hot or at room temperature. It lasts five days in the refrigerator or one month in the freezer.

'UN-FRIED' RICE
CHĀHAN FŪ TAKIKOMI GOHAN 炒飯風炊き込みご飯

SERVES 3–4

This is a variation of takikomi gohan that uses common fried rice ingredients to create something that is kinda-sorta like fried rice, but not fried. Let me be clear: this isn't *really* a replacement for fried rice, but it does the job if you're not in the mood to wash up two pans.

Pour the just-boiled water over the mushrooms and leave to rehydrate for at least 15 minutes while you prepare the rest of the dish. Wash the rice and place it in a rice cooker or saucepan along with the chicken stock powder, sesame oil and salt. Squeeze the mushrooms dry and combine the liquid with the mirin, soy sauce and sake. Add enough water to make a total of 390 g (13¾ oz). Pour this over the rice, then scatter the vegetables over the top, followed by the prawns and meat. Crack the eggs into a bowl (to catch any errant bits of shell), then put these in the pan as well. Cook according to the instructions on page 27. When the rice is finished cooking, break up the eggs and fold everything together. Serve hot or at room temperature. It lasts five days in the refrigerator or one month in the freezer.

100 ml (3½ fl oz/scant ½ cup)
   just-boiled water
4 (6–8 g/¼–⅓ oz) dried
   shiitake mushrooms
300 g (10½ oz/2 rice cooker cups) rice
1 teaspoon chicken stock powder
1 teaspoon sesame oil
¼ teaspoon salt
1 tablespoon mirin
1 tablespoon soy sauce
1 tablespoon sake
1 small or ½ medium carrot, peeled
   and finely diced
1 baby leek, diced
2 garlic cloves, finely sliced
1 cm (½ in) fresh ginger root, peeled
   and finely chopped
20 g (¾ oz) bamboo shoots, finely
   chopped (optional)
80 g (3 oz) raw shelled prawns (shrimp),
   roughly chopped
60 g (2 oz) pork or chicken, finely sliced
2 eggs

SMOKED SALMON AND SEAWEED RICE
SUMŌKU SĀMON KAISŌ MESHI スモークサーモン海藻飯

SERVES **3–4** OR MAKES **6** ONIGIRI; COULD ALSO SERVE **2–3** AS A ONE-DISH MEAL

300 g (10½ oz/2 rice cooker cups) rice
1 cm (½ in) fresh ginger root, washed
 and finely sliced
1½ tablespoons sesame seeds
½ teaspoon dashi powder
¼ teaspoon salt
2 teaspoons soy sauce
2 teaspoons mirin
2 teaspoons sake
390 g (13¾ oz) water
a few drops of sesame oil
2 tablespoons dried wakame
80 g (3 oz) hot-smoked salmon
 (or any salmon, boneless and skinless)
1 tablespoon aonori flakes

This is a one-pot rice recipe based on one of my favourite varieties of conbini onigiri, made with salmon, *wakame* (a type of sea vegetable) and sesame seeds. This version uses hot-smoked salmon, which is not traditional, but I love the way the smoked fish echoes the flavour in dashi.

Wash the rice and combine in a rice cooker or saucepan along with the other ingredients, except the wakame, salmon and aonori. Sit the wakame and salmon on top of the mixed rice and cook everything according to the instructions on page 27. When the rice is done, remove the ginger, sprinkle over the aonori and fold it in, breaking up the salmon as you go. Serve at any temperature. It lasts four days in the refrigerator or one month in the freezer.

CELERY WITH UMEBOSHI PASTE AND WHITE SESAME
SERORI NO NERIUME AE セロリの胡麻と練り梅和え

SERVES **4–6**

2 celery stalks, trimmed
2 teaspoons umeboshi paste
1 teaspoon sugar
1 teaspoon sesame seeds

Celery makes an excellent pickle. With its vaguely bitter flavour and watery crunch, it's innately quite refreshing, I think. Add to that some sharply salty-sour *umeboshi* (Japanese pickled plums) and you've got a real punchy pickle there. There is a word in Korean for dishes like this – *bap doduk*: 'rice thief' – because it is so irresistibly, mouth-wateringly tangy, it'll have you returning to your rice so rapidly that you'll end up wondering where it all went.

Slice the celery very thinly at a sharp angle, so you have slices that are about 4 cm (1½ in) long but no thicker than 2 mm (⅛ in). Toss these with the umeboshi, sugar and sesame until the celery is well coated. You can keep these in the refrigerator for a few days, but the salt from the umeboshi will start to draw liquid out of the celery and make the dressing watery. It will still taste fine, but I prefer to eat these fresh.

EXTRA-NUTTY BROWN RICE

NŌKŌ NA KAORI NO GENMAI 濃厚な香りの玄米

SERVES 4

1 tablespoon red miso
700 g (1 lb 9 oz) water
300 g (10½ oz/2 rice cooker cups)
    genmai (Japanese brown rice)
1 tablespoon soy sauce
¼ teaspoon salt
¼ teaspoon MSG
a few drops of sesame oil
5 g (¼ oz) butter

White, Japanese, short-grain rice is my one true rice love, but sometimes I do enjoy the nutty flavour and bouncy chew of brown rice. I was going to include a basic 'how-to' recipe, but the back of the box has that covered (and it works). Instead, here is a seasoned brown rice recipe with a little twist in the method that enhances its natural nuttiness for, like, über-nuttiness. The extra ingredients also make the rice stickier, so it's easier to eat with chopsticks.

The same rules for white rice also apply to brown rice: it has to be Japanese short-grain, it should be washed a few times and, if you're going to have it later, chill it quickly and keep it in the refrigerator or freezer.

Mix the miso with a little of the water to make a smooth, thin paste. Wash the rice and transfer to a medium saucepan with the other ingredients, as well as the diluted miso and remaining water. Bring to the boil and then put a lid on and reduce the heat to as low as your hob goes. Leave to simmer and steam for 35 minutes, then remove the lid. Turn the heat all the way back up and cook for another few minutes so the bottom begins to brown and caramelise. You won't be able to see what's going on, so you have to rely on your nose; at first, you will notice a sweet 'buttered popcorn' aroma, followed by a 'roasted hazelnut' aroma. After a minute or two, you should smell a distinct caramel scent – at which point, turn the heat off, put the lid back on the pan and leave to rest for at least 10 minutes (but 20 is better). Gently stir the rice before serving. Serve the rice hot or at room temperature. It lasts four days in the refrigerator or one month in the freezer.

NOTE If you are using a rice cooker, follow its instructions and the water level indicated for brown rice, but include the seasonings as written. If your rice cooker has a 'crust' function, use it; otherwise, when the rice is done, tip it out into a frying pan (skillet) and cook over a high heat to develop the nutty flavour.

SEA BREAM RICE
TAI MESHI 鯛めし

SERVES 4 AS A SIDE DISH; **2–3** IF YOU'RE HAVING IT ON ITS OWN

Tai meshi, or sea bream rice, is a perennially popular preparation of (you guessed it) sea bream and rice. There are many variations, including an unusual version from the city of Uwajima in Ehime prefecture (Japan's largest producer of sea bream) in which sea bream sashimi is eaten with egg yolk on warm rice. While that sounds delicious, most tai meshi takes the form of takikomi gohan where the fish and rice are cooked together. This is a lovely side dish, a meal on its own and a show-stopper for entertaining – bring the dish to the table, sea bream still intact atop the rice, then mix it up and serve it to your guests. This can be made with a whole bream to add a deeper flavour to the rice and a great visual impact, but frankly it is a pain to then bone the fish, so personally I prefer fillets.

Preheat the grill (broiler) to high and dry the skin of the sea bream with paper towel. Grease a baking sheet and place the bream on it, skin-side up. Grill (broil) the bream for about 5 minutes until the skin is browned. Wash the rice and combine in a rice cooker or saucepan with the ginger and seasonings. Lay the bream on top of the rice, then cook everything together according to the instructions on page 27. When the rice is done, sprinkle over the chopped herbs and fold them into the rice, breaking up the bream as you go. Serve hot. This lasts four days in the refrigerator or one month in the freezer.

2 × 200 g (7 oz) sea bream fillets, scaled and boned
vegetable oil, for greasing
300 g (10½ oz/2 rice cooker cups) rice
2 cm (¾ in) fresh ginger root, washed, peeled and very thinly julienned
1 tablespoon sake
2 teaspoons soy sauce
1 teaspoon mirin
¼ teaspoon salt
360 g (12⅔ oz) dashi
handful of flat-leaf parsley leaves or pea shoots, finely chopped

CRAB, SWEETCORN AND SPRING ONION RICE

TŌMOROKOSHI TO NEGI NO KANIMESHI とうもろこしとネギの蟹飯

SERVES 3–4 OR MAKES **6** ONIGIRI; COULD ALSO SERVE **2–3** AS A ONE-DISH MEAL

300 g (10½ oz/2 rice cooker cups) rice
¼ teaspoon salt
1 tablespoon soy sauce
1 tablespoon mirin
1 tablespoon sake
1 tin (150–200 g/5–7 oz undrained weight)
    of sweetcorn
4 spring onions (scallions)
100 g (3½ oz) fake crab, roughly chopped,
    or real white crab meat, flaked
1 tablespoon aonori flakes

Fake crab is underrated. It gets a bad rap and, no, of course it's not as good as the real thing, but if you're just after flaky, seafoody protein and a sweet, crabby flavour, then it certainly does the job. It is also in no way inauthentic – fake crab, or *kanikama*, is everywhere in Japan. There's even an artisanal version called *kaoribako*, which is made with a less fluorescent pink colouring and a finer grain that really does give it an uncanny resemblance to real crab. You can buy a similar product here in the UK too, called 'surimi royale', the Cadillac of imitation seafood products. But whatever *surimi* you can get will be good, as will real crab, if you're feeling fancy!

Wash the rice and place in a rice cooker or saucepan along with the salt. Combine the soy sauce, mirin, sake and liquid from the tin of sweetcorn in a measuring jug, then addenough water so that the total liquid comes to 390 g (13¾ oz). Pour this into the rice cooker or saucepan. Roughly chop the white parts of the spring onions and finely slice the green parts. Place the green parts in a container, cover with cold water and keep in the refrigerator until the rice is done cooking. Scatter the white parts of the spring onions, the corn and the crab over the rice, then cook everything according to the instructions on page 27. When the rice is done, drain the green parts of the spring onion, sprinkle them over the rice along with the aonori and fold everything together. Serve hot or at room temperature. It lasts four days in the refrigerator or one month in the freezer.

CLAM RICE

ASARI GOHAN あさりご飯

SERVES 4

This recipe is inspired by Fukagawa-meshi, an East Tokyo speciality that makes the most of the little clams that live in Tokyo Bay by using both their meat and their juice to flavour rice and miso soup. Fresh or frozen clams are fine, just make sure you buy good-quality clams that are free of grit. Mussels work well too. For me, *tsukudani* or similar sweet pickles are a must with this – try it with the cockle tsukudani (page 56) for a double-bivalve hit.

If you're using fresh clams, discard any with broken shells or any open ones that don't close when you tap them hard. If you're using frozen clams, don't thaw them – they'll open when you do and you'll lose their juice.

Place the sake in a saucepan and bring to a simmer. Tip in the spring onions, ginger and clams and place a lid on the pan. Bring to the boil and then steam for about 5 minutes, shaking the pan occasionally, until all of the clams have opened and the meat has cooked through. Pass the broth through a sieve and reserve. When the clams are cool enough to handle, pick the meat from them and reserve separately, along with as much of the spring onions and ginger as you can salvage.

Wash the rice and place in a saucepan or rice cooker. Combine the reserved clam broth with the miso, sugar and dashi powder in a measuring jug, mix well to dissolve, then add enough water to make a total of 400 g (14 oz). Add to the rice and cook according to the instructions on page 27.

When the rice has finished cooking, fold back in the clam meat and vegetables, along with the pea shoots, if using. Serve hot or at room temperature, with pickles. It lasts five days in the refrigerator or one month in the freezer.

500 g (1 lb 2 oz) clams in their shells, cleaned
4 tablespoons sake
2 spring onions (scallions), finely sliced
   at an angle
1 cm (½ in) fresh ginger root, peeled
   and finely shredded
300 g (10½ oz/2 rice cooker cups) rice
1 tablespoon miso
1 teaspoon sugar
½ teaspoon dashi powder
handful of pea shoots, chopped (optional)

THE NOTORIOUS TKG
TAMAGO KAKE GOHAN 卵かけご飯

SERVES 2

a few drops of sesame oil
2 tablespoons plus a few drops of soy sauce
2 eggs
2 portions of freshly cooked or freshly
    reheated rice
10 g (½ oz) butter (optional)
pickles, as needed (any kind, but I like
    something spicy like kimchi or *spicy
    pickled bok choy*, page 66)
1 pack (about 10 sheets) of Korean nori,
    or 2 sheets of Japanese nori, each cut
    into 6 small rectangles

I wasn't quite sure where to put this recipe, because, well, it's hardly a recipe, and more a bowl of rice with something on top. But like nattō (pages 58–61), it is such a massively popular breakfast item in Japan, I had to include it. TKG, short for *tamago kake gohan*, is raw egg with soy sauce on rice. That's it. The egg can be beaten, or not. The soy sauce can be mixed with the egg, or just poured over. Sometimes, only the yolk is used, or it could be a slow-cooked, soft-set *onsen* egg. It is a simple, delicious, pure 1-2-3 punch of carbs, protein and salt. Of course, embellishments abound in Japan; the Japanese recipe site Macaro-ni.jp has a roundup of 30 different TKG arrangements that include spicy miso sauce, tempura scraps and a 'carbonara' TKG, in which the egg is joined by bacon, pepper and Parmesan. The TKG I usually make is nothing so extravagant, but it is a little different from the most basic version; and honestly, it is one of my all-time favourite mouthfuls.

Use the sesame oil to lightly grease two small ramekins or similar. Add a few drops of soy sauce to each ramekin. Separate the eggs and put the yolks in the prepared ramekins. Beat the whites with the remaining 2 tablespoons of soy sauce. When the rice has finished cooking or reheating and is piping hot, fold the whites into the rice along with the butter, if using. They will cook lightly in the residual heat and form a sort of sticky egg glaze. To serve, pile the rice into bowls and slip the egg yolks on top. To eat, break the yolks and use chopsticks to pack some eggy rice and pickles into each little square of nori, like little parcels or hand rolls. Eat each little roll as soon as you make it, so the nori remains crunchy and crisp.

YUZU-PICKLED FENNEL

YUZU FŪMI FENERU NO AMAZU-ZUKE ゆず風味フェネルの甘酢漬け

SERVES 8–10

Fennel and yuzu are a wonderful combination, with each ingredient making the other even more aromatic and uplifting. But this yuzu-infused sweet vinegar brine works with all kinds of other vegetables as well – try it with small turnips, carrots, courgettes or watermelon rinds. Yuzu zest is admittedly hard to find – out of season, you can get it frozen or dried, but frozen is very much preferable if you can get it. Otherwise, any good, aromatic citrus peel will do.

Combine everything except the fennel in a small saucepan and warm over a medium-high heat until just below simmering – you want to get it just hot enough to dissolve the sugar and salt and infuse the citrus. Do not boil or you will start to lose the aroma. Leave the brine to cool, then cut the fennel in half and slice it thinly, top-to-tail rather than across the grain. Pack the fennel into a sterilised jar and pour over the brine, ensuring the fennel is totally submerged. Screw the lid on. Leave to pickle in the refrigerator for at least a day, and up to a month.

200 ml (7 fl oz/scant 1 cup) vinegar
4 tablespoons water
40 g (1½ oz) caster (superfine) sugar
1 tablespoon yuzu zest (or similar citrus zest), shredded
1 teaspoon salt
1 teaspoon yuzu juice (or similar)
1 very small pinch of chilli (hot pepper) flakes (optional)
½ teaspoon dashi powder (optional)
1 medium-sized bulb (about 300 g/ 10½ oz) of fennel

SOY-CANDIED COCKLES

ZARUGAI NO TSUKUDANI ざる貝の佃煮

SERVES 10–12

200 g (7 oz) cockle meat (fresh or frozen,
    not in vinegar or brine)
4 tablespoons soy sauce
3 tablespoons dark brown sugar
3 tablespoons mirin
2 tablespoons sake

Tsukudani is here in the pickle section, but is it a pickle? It isn't soured by vinegar or fermentation, but it is preserved, and it occupies a similar sort of space as pickles in Japanese meals: as a strongly-flavoured side, or as something to enliven rice. But tsukudani (named for Tsukuda, the area of Tokyo in which its production began) is more like a jam – a salty, salty jam. Basically, this method of preservation involves boiling various ingredients, typically seaweeds and seafood, in a mixture of sugar, mirin, sake and soy sauce until everything reduces down to a syrupy, blackish mass of concentrated deliciousness. I made this cockle tsukudani for the first time a few years ago and served it to an actual cockle farmer in Essex. His assessment: 'They taste like cockle liquorice.' This was not intended as a compliment. But I don't care – these are sweet, glistening jewels of intense, meaty shellfish flavour and I won't hear a bad word about them. Just a little spoonful on a bowl of hot rice; I am in liquoricey cockle heaven!

Combine all of the ingredients in a saucepan along with enough water to cover by about 2.5 cm (1 in). Bring to the boil and then keep boiling, stirring occasionally, until the liquid reduces all the way down to virtually nothing, with the consistency of a very thick syrup. At the end of this process, you should stir it more frequently to prevent burning. When the liquid is thick and jammy, remove from the pan and leave to cool before packing into a sterilised jar and keeping in the refrigerator for up to one month. Serve at any temperature.

THREE WAYS WITH NATTŌ

NATTŌ NO ARENJI SANSEN 納豆のアレンジ3選

SERVES 1–2

When I lived in Japan, one of the most common questions I was asked whenever the conversation turned to food (which happened a lot) was 'Can you eat nattō?' The question was sort of a test, and sort of a tease, because people in Japan know that nattō is something foreigners often find somewhat challenging.

For the uninitiated, nattō are fermented soybeans with a nutty, slightly cheesy flavour and a texture described as *nebaneba* in Japanese – sticky and slippery, a bit like okra – a mouthfeel that is treasured in Japan, but much less familiar in European cookery. But honestly, nattō is much more delicious and less weird than its reputation suggests, and besides, it's so popular as a breakfast item in Japan that I simply couldn't write a book that touches on Japanese breakfasts without including it.

Personally, I have always enjoyed the smell and the flavour of nattō. I think it's pleasantly nutty and beany; I once heard the aroma described as a bit like coffee, which I think is accurate. I'm less fond of its sticky texture, but I have acquired the taste for that, too. In Japan, I ate nattō on a regular basis, though mainly for its purported health benefits. My friend Kazumi told me that eating nattō every night before I went to bed would give me more energy in the mornings – I have never been a morning person, so this appealed to me. (I don't recall if it actually worked, but I do remember it gave me some weird dreams.)

Particularly if you're a nattō novice, I think it's best if you have it with something else, either for contrast, or just to take the edge off its intrinsic nattō-ness. Here are three of my favourite ways to jazz up nattō in the mornings, which may even convince the nattō sceptics among you.

Nattō is sold frozen at East Asian supermarkets – thaw it out in the refrigerator overnight before eating, and once it's thawed, eat it within a couple of days.

PICKLES

SMALL SIDES

'DANISH HOT DOG' NATTŌ

SERVES 1

1 pack of nattō
big pinch of finely chopped onion,
    spring onion (scallion) or chives
1 small chunk of gherkin (cornichon)
    or other kind of pickled cucumber,
    finely chopped
1 tablespoon crispy fried onions
    (shop-bought is fine)

This idea came to me after having nattō one morning topped with some crispy onions, which I'd bought to make Danish hot dogs the week before. Some of the key toppings for Danish hot dogs, such as crispy onions, raw onions, pickled cucumbers and mustard, are great with nattō – in fact, spring onions and mustard are traditional toppings anyway, and most nattō already comes packaged with a little sachet of mustard.

Stir the onion and pickles into the nattō along with the mustard and tsuyu from the nattō packet. Garnish with the fried onions and eat with rice or with bread.

PICKLES

SMALL SIDES

KIMCHI SESAME NATTŌ

SERVES 1

1 tablespoon kimchi, roughly chopped
a few drops of sesame oil
1 pack of nattō
pinch of sesame seeds

The vibrant sour-spicy flavour and crisp texture of kimchi provide a perfect contrast to nattō, while sesame brings out its nutty flavour.

Stir the kimchi and sesame oil into the nattō along with the mustard and tsuyu from the nattō packet. Garnish with the sesame and eat with rice or in a sandwich.

NATTŌST

SERVES 1–2

Japanese breakfasts are often a mash-up of domestic and international items, and one of the most popular breakfast fusion items is nattō toast, which for me is ingenious, because it provides a lovely crunch to interrupt the nattō's gooey texture. In Japan, it is common to top nattō toast with melted cheese, which is never a bad idea.

Toast the bread to your liking. Stir the spring onion and Worcestershire sauce into the nattō along with the mustard and tsuyu from the nattō packet. Thinly spread the butter and miso on the toast, then spread the nattō on top. Cover with the grated cheese (if using) and grill (broil) until it melts.

1 slice of bread
½ spring onion (scallion), finely sliced
1 dash of Worcestershire sauce
1 pack of nattō
small pat of butter
1 teaspoon miso
handful of grated cheese (optional)

SMOKY PICKLED DAIKON

IBURIGAKKO FŪ DAIKON TSUKEMONO いぶりがっこ風大根漬物

SERVES 10

One of the most unique types of Japanese pickles is *iburigakko*, a speciality of Akita prefecture. Typically, most daikon is air-dried before pickling in Japan, which concentrates their flavour and allows them to absorb more of the pickling medium. However, Akita is located on the far northern end of Honshu, where the air is too cold and damp to effectively air-dry daikon, so people there began the practice of hanging daikon to dry indoors, high above traditional wood-burning hearths called *irori*. The warm currents from the fire allow the daikon to dry efficiently and, at the same time, they pick up a rich, smoky flavour from the wood. The daikon is then pickled in a bed of cultured rice bran, a traditional method called *nukazuke*.

This process is, quite frankly, completely unachievable for all but the most ambitious home cooks. However, you can get a sort of similar smoky-funky flavour from brining the daikon with lapsang souchong tea, which I have used for years to impart a smoked note to marinated eggs. The end result cannot be called iburigakko, but it's very delicious – a particularly good accompaniment to eggs or rich meats.

If your daikon is quite big, say, larger than 5 cm (2 in in diameter, cut it in half lengthwise to make two half-cylindrical chunks. Place the daikon on a rack in a fan oven set to 100°C (210°F/gas ½) and leave to dry for 3 hours. Meanwhile, make the brine by warming the dashi, sake, sugar, salt and tea together in a saucepan to a gentle simmer. Remove from the heat and leave to infuse for 5–10 minutes – the longer you leave the tea, the smokier the flavour will be. Remove the tea (use a sieve if you're using loose leaf tea), then stir in the soy sauce, vinegar and miso. When the daikon has finished drying – it should be shrivelled, a bit limp and lightly browned – submerge in the brine and leave to pickle in the refrigerator for at least a day, but give it a week if you can. To serve, remove from the brine and cut into slices about 5 mm (¼ in) thick. This lasts up to a year in the refrigerator.

200 g (7 oz) chunk of daikon, unpeeled but scrubbed clean and patted dry
100 ml (3½ fl oz/scant ½ cup) dashi
3 tablespoons sake
2 tablespoons sugar
½ tablespoon salt
2 tea bags/5 g (¼ oz) lapsang souchong tea
3 tablespoons soy sauce
3 tablespoons vinegar
1 tablespoon red miso

MISO-PICKLED GARLIC
NINNIKU NO MISOZUKE にんにくの味噌漬け

SERVES 6

2 garlic bulbs, separated into cloves,
    skin on
100 g (3½ oz) red miso
2 tablespoons dark brown sugar
1 tablespoon sake
½ teaspoon shichimi pepper (optional)

The deliciousness of garlic pickled in miso is self-explanatory. It's garlic. It's miso. It's fantastic. But actually, it is more than the sum of its parts – a kind of alchemy occurs as the garlic hibernates in its bed of miso, making its flavour somehow both more mellow and more concentrated. Plus, you end up with garlic miso as a by-product, which tastes great in pretty much any recipe that calls for plain miso, especially if they involve red meat or shellfish. This will be ready to eat after a week, but the longer you leave it, the more delicious it will become. I once had garlic that had been pickling in miso for over a year – the result was like some kind of gorgeous garlic caramel.

Bring a medium saucepan of water to the boil. Blanch the garlic cloves in the pan, still in their skin, for 30 seconds, then transfer to a bowl of cold water to stop them cooking. (This will make the garlic easier to peel and removes some of their harsh raw flavour.) Peel the garlic and set aside. Combine the miso, sugar, sake, shichimi (if using) and the garlic. Mix well and pack everything into a sterilised jar, and put a piece of cling film (plastic wrap) directly onto the surface of the miso-garlic mixture to keep it from drying out. Put the lid on the jar and leave at room temperature for at least two weeks, but it is better if you can leave it for a month or longer – the garlic will become softer and more mellow. This lasts up to a year in the refrigerator.

PICKLES

SPICY PICKLED PAK CHOI
CHINGENSAI NO KARASHIZUKE チンゲン菜の辛子漬け

SERVES 10

10 g (½ oz) salt
500 g (1 lb 2 oz) pak choi (bok choi),
 washed and cut into roughly 2.5 cm
 (1 in) chunks
3 garlic cloves, finely grated
2 tablespoons Korean chilli powder
2 tablespoons soy sauce
2 tablespoons sesame seeds
1 teaspoon sugar
1 teaspoon sesame oil
½ teaspoon wasabi (optional)
¼ teaspoon MSG

One of my all-time favourite Japanese pickles is *karashi takana,* or spicy pickled mustard greens. These are especially delicious on garlicky Kumamoto ramen, but they're also great on their own or with plain rice. Mustard greens are a little difficult to find, but you can achieve a similar flavour and texture by using pak choi instead. The result is something a bit like kimchi, but with an earthier flavour and a subtle mustardy aroma.

Massage the salt into the pak choi and leave to wilt for about 20 minutes. Squeeze the pak choi to wring out as much liquid as you can (save the liquid!). Wait another 20 minutes, then wring out the liquid once again. Mix in all the remaining ingredients, then pack everything tightly into a sterilised jar, so the liquid rises above the surface of the pak choi (it needs to be completely submerged in order to prevent spoilage). Put the lid on the jar, but don't screw it on tightly, to let carbon dioxide escape as it ferments. Leave at room temperature for at least three days and up to a week, or possibly longer if you like very sour pickles or if your kitchen is on the cold side. Taste the pickles periodically and transfer to the refrigerator when they are acidic enough for you. Once fully fermented, these will keep in the refrigerator for up to a year.

ご飯物 漬物 汁物

SCOTCH BONNET-PICKLED BAMBOO SHOOTS

MENMA NO GEKIKARA SUKOCCHI BONETTO ZUKE メンマの激辛スコッチボネット漬け

SERVES **10,** PERHAPS FEWER IF YOU ARE A MASOCHIST

150–200 g (5–7 oz) *menma*
    (Japanese seasoned bamboo shoots),
    undrained weight
3 tablespoons soy sauce
10 g (½ oz) Scotch bonnet chillies,
    destemmed and roughly chopped

These little firecrackers were one of our key garnishes at the restaurant, a secret weapon that could be used to enliven any dish and shock any customer with their lightning strike of fruity heat. I suppose they fall squarely into the 'inauthentic' camp, as few Japanese pickles are spicy, and none are *this* spicy. But still, I had to include them because nothing wakes me up quite like a couple of these. They are very good on ramen, of course, but also with any rich, meaty dishes, like pork donburi (page 154) or *mābō nasu* (page 112).

Combine the bamboo shoots' brine, soy sauce and Scotch bonnets in a blender and purée until smooth. Pour this mixture back over the bamboo shoots and mix well. Leave to marinate for a few hours before eating. This lasts two weeks in the refrigerator.

SALTED CHINESE LEAF WITH SANSHŌ

SANSHŌ IRI SHIOZUKE HAKUSAI 山椒入り塩漬け白菜

SERVES 4–6

Perhaps the simplest mode of Japanese pickling is *shiozuke*, or salt-pickling. In fact, sometimes these aren't really pickles at all, in the sense that they are not preserved; vegetables are often salted, wilted and drained, and eaten as is. The salt acts more as a seasoning and a firming agent, as opposed to a medium for fermentation. However, shiozuke pickles can be packed into containers and left longer. This recipe lets you choose how pickley you'd like your pickles to be.

One of the most common vegetables to be prepared as shiozuke is *hakusai*, or Chinese leaf. This is often accented with something aromatic, such as yuzu or ginger. For this recipe, I've chosen *sanshō*, the Japanese cultivar of Sichuan pepper, which is not spicy but has an enlivening tingle and bright, lemongrassy aroma.

Massage the salt into the cabbage and leave to wilt for about 20 minutes. Squeeze the cabbage to wring out the liquid. If you plan to eat this immediately, without pickling, simply discard the liquid, stir in the sanshō and enjoy. If you'd like the cabbage to sour, stir the sanshō through the cabbage and its liquid, then pack everything tightly into a sterilised jar, so the liquid rises above the surface of the cabbage (it needs to be completely submerged in order to prevent spoilage). Put the lid on the jar, but don't screw it on tightly, to let carbon dioxide escape as it ferments. Leave at room temperature for anywhere from one day to a week, possibly longer if you like very sour pickles or if your kitchen is on the cold side. Taste the pickles periodically and transfer to the refrigerator when they are acidic enough for you. You can serve this cold or at room temperature. Lightly fermented pickles should be eaten within a few days; very sour ones will last for several months.

300 g (10½ oz) Chinese leaf (napa cabbage), cut into roughly 1 cm (½ in) chunks
1 teaspoon salt
¼ teaspoon ground sanshō pepper

CLEAR SOUP WITH CRAB AND PARSLEY

KANI TO PASERI NO SUIMONO 蟹とパセリの吸い物

SERVES 4

700 ml (24 fl oz/scant 3 cups) dashi
1 tablespoon sake
1 tablespoon soy sauce
½ teaspoon salt
100 g (3½ oz) picked white crab meat –
    if you can use chunks of whole leg or
    claw that would make this extra elegant
a few shreds of yuzu or lime zest
flat-leaf parsley leaves or coriander,
    to garnish

I am not an elegant person. Even when I make an effort, I'm always slightly dishevelled, and that goes for my food, too. But that doesn't mean I don't like nice things. In fact, I have a real affection for the understated and refined side of Japanese aesthetics, like Bashō's classic haiku below, or the simple but profound soups that contain just a few ingredients but deliver rolling waves of flavour. Shizuo Tsuji writes a delightful ode to these simple soups in *Japanese Cooking: A Simple Art,* which I encourage you to read. Soups such as this one – with a few fresh green leaves floating on the surface like lily pads, hiding the pile of sweet crab meat below – always puts me in a poetic mood, too.

Combine the dashi, sake, soy sauce and salt in a saucepan and bring to a simmer. Divide the crab meat as neat, compact mounds into four bowls, and add the citrus zest and parsley around each mound. Carefully pour the seasoned dashi into each bowl so you do not disturb the crab. Place saucers or lids on each bowl so the crab warms through from the steam and serve immediately. This lasts five days in the refrigerator, but is best eaten fresh.

An old soup bowl
Remove the lid –
The scent of crab!

ANDERSON

The old pond
A frog jumps in –
The sound of water!

BASHŌ

HOMEMADE INSTANT MISO SOUP
OUCHI DE TSUKURU INSUTANTO MISOJIRU お家で作るインスタント味噌汁

SERVES 4–5

'Don't make it if you can buy it.' This is one of my rules to live by. While I have some admiration for people who, say, make their own croissants from scratch, it's like ... do they not know they can *buy* croissants? Croissants from a bakery are fantastic!

So, by the same logic, you shouldn't make your own instant miso soup as it is widely available and tasty... *or is it*? I am a huge instant miso soup fan but, in this case, shop-bought is not as good as homemade. It is also more expensive, and *only just* easier. You can bash this instant miso soup mix together along with some prepared toppings in about 10 minutes and then it's good to go, ready to be reconstituted with hot water in seconds flat. And the main benefit of making your own is that it's fully customisable – you can use all kinds of interesting miso varieties, blend them to your liking and add whatever other ingredients you like – I've listed some suggestions at the end of the ingredients list, but that's just to get you started.

Simply stir together all of the ingredients until smooth and well-mixed. To make miso soup, use 1 slightly heaped tablespoon per bowl and add 150–170 ml (5–6 fl oz/scant ⅔–¾ cup) of just-boiled water, depending on how salty and strong you like it, along with whatever prepared toppings you like. Give everything a little stir and, if you are using dried products (such as wakame), give them a minute to plump up before tucking in. Always serve hot. Undiluted, this lasts for a week in the refrigerator.

The suggested toppings should be kept separate from the miso mixture until ready to serve. If you are packing miso soup for lunch, put the miso mix and the toppings in separate small containers.

70 g (2½ oz) miso
1 teaspoon dashi powder
1 tablespoon mirin
½ teaspoon water

Suggested (per bowl):

2 pinches of wakame, hijiki or similar
   dried seaweed
small chunk (5 g/¼ oz or so) of aburaage
   or similar fried tofu, diced
20 g (¾ oz) silken tofu, diced
2 spring onions (scallions) or chives,
   finely chopped
pinch of sesame seeds
small handful of cooked prawns (shrimps),
   scallops or other shellfish
small handful of spinach, pea shoots,
   flat-leaf parsley leaves or other
   tender leaves
small handful of dried glass noodles,
   or a little nest of instant ramen

BEETROOT MISO SOUP

BĪTSU NO MISOSHIRU ビーツの味噌汁

SERVES 4

1 small onion, cut into 1 cm (½ in) cubes
250 g (9 oz) cooked beetroot (beet),
    peeled and cut into 1 cm (½ in) cubes
550 ml (19 fl oz/2⅓ cups) dashi
50 g (2 oz) miso (or more or less, to taste)
½ teaspoon wasabi (optional)
black pepper, to taste
flat-leaf parsley leaves, to garnish

This recipe was inspired by Yoko Inagaki, who runs the Osaka Kitchen cookery school in Osaka. In 2020, she challenged herself to make a different bowl of miso soup every day for 100 days, and she posted all of them on Instagram. Her creativity was astounding: wild boar miso soup; tomato, mozzarella and cricket miso soup; KFC and rosemary miso soup; curry miso soup; and tom yum kung miso soup, along with more traditional versions including clams, baby sardines, oysters and seasonal vegetables. They all looked fantastic, but the one I kept thinking about was one Yoko made with beetroot and sour cream; pink to raise awareness for breast cancer. I've always loved beetroot and miso together, so I knew I had to make my own. Yoko's original uses potato and butter, but I've gone with more of a straight beetroot and miso flavour profile, plus a bit of wasabi – beetroot and horseradish are a classic combination after all.

Combine the onion, beetroot and dashi in a saucepan and bring to the boil for about 15 minutes until the onion is very soft. Remove from the heat, then scoop roughly half the beetroot and onion out of the broth with a slotted spoon and set aside. Add the miso, wasabi and pepper to the soup, then blend to a smooth purée with a blender. Add the diced onion and beetroot back to the soup and return to a low simmer. Ladle into soup bowls, garnish with the parsley and serve while hot. This lasts four days in the refrigerator.

CHICKEN, ROOT VEGETABLE AND PEARL BARLEY MISO SOUP

TORI-JIRU 鶏汁

SERVES 4 AS A STARTER OR SIDE, OR 2 AS A MAIN

20 g (¾ oz) pearl barley, cooked
    (see method)
1 chicken drumstick or thigh, boned,
    cut into 2.5 cm (1 in) chunks
½ onion, diced
1 garlic clove, finely chopped
5 g (¼ oz) fresh ginger root, peeled
    and finely shredded
600 ml (20 fl oz/2½ cups) dashi
    or chicken stock
50 g (2 oz) daikon, peeled and cut into
    wedges about 5 mm (¼ in) thick,
    or radishes, washed and quartered
70–80 g (2½–3 oz) burdock, Jerusalem
    artichokes or parsnips, peeled and
    cut into 1 cm (½ in) cubes
1 small carrot, peeled and cut into
    semi-circles about 5 mm (¼ in) thick
60 g (2 oz) miso
1 spring onion (scallion), finely sliced
shichimi pepper or chilli oil, to taste
    (optional)

One of my all-time favourite Japanese comfort foods is *tonjiru*, a hearty miso soup made with chunky root vegetables and slow-cooked pork. This recipe is based on that, but uses chicken instead of pork for a lighter flavour but no less heart-warming effect. Like any good chicken soup, this one also works as a meal in and of itself.

Cooking times for pearl barley seem to vary widely depending on what kind you buy, so it's best to cook it ahead of time according to the package instructions. Once it's done, rinse it under cold water and set aside.

    Place the chicken, onion, garlic, ginger and dashi together in a saucepan and bring to a low boil. Use a small sieve or ladle to remove any scum that forms on the surface. Boil for about 15 minutes, then add the daikon, burdock and carrot, and continue cooking for another 15 minutes until the vegetables and chicken are very soft. Top up the water periodically so the broth doesn't reduce. Add the cooked pearl barley and simmer for a few minutes, then remove from the heat and whisk in the miso and spring onion. Serve hot with shichimi or chilli oil, if using. This lasts four days in the refrigerator.

SHIMEJI MUSHROOM AND OKRA MISO SOUP

NAMEKO JIRU FŪ SHIMEJI TO OKURA NO MISOSHIRU なめこ汁風しめじとオクラの味噌汁

SERVES 4

700 ml (24 fl oz/scant 3 cups) dashi
2.5 cm (1 in) piece of leek, finely sliced
100 g (3½ oz) shimeji mushrooms,
　　root ends removed and roughly chopped
80 g (3 oz) okra, stems removed and
　　roughly chopped
60 g (2 oz) red miso
120 g (4 oz) firm silken tofu, cubed

One of the most popular variations of miso soup in Japan is made with a type of mushroom called *nameko*, which has a mellow, nutty flavour and an unusual coating of slippery goo – another example of Japan's treasured nebaneba mouthfeel. When cooked in soup, this goo thickens the broth, making for a full-bodied, lip-sticking, hearty miso soup. You can achieve a similar effect using a combination of *shimeji* mushrooms (also known as beech mushrooms) and okra.

Combine the dashi, leek and mushrooms in a saucepan, then bring to the boil. Reduce the heat to a high simmer and cook for 5 minutes. Add the okra and cook for another 3–4 minutes, then remove from the heat and whisk in the miso. Finally, add the tofu and bring the soup back to a simmer before serving. This lasts five days in the refrigerator.

CLEAR SOUP WITH RADISHES, THIN NOODLES AND PONZU

PONZU AJI NO RADISSHU TO HARUSAME SŪPU ポン酢味のラディッシュと春雨スープ

SERVES **4**

80 g (3 oz) radishes
700 ml (24 fl oz/scant 3 cups) dashi
    (kombu dashi is a good choice for this,
    and it makes it vegan)
5 tablespoons ponzu
30 g (1 oz) glass noodles or sōmen,
    broken into small pieces
salt, to taste
handful of chives, cut into 1 cm
    (½ in) lengths

This recipe is inspired by a Nissin instant udon product designed to fit into a miso soup bowl, so it can be had alongside other things, or as a soupy snack rather than a full meal. I like it because it's yummy, but also because it's a nice change from the usual miso. The refreshing aroma of *ponzu* keeps this soup lovely and light, while glass noodles (or thin wheat noodles called *sōmen*) add a bit of substance without making it heavy. The radishes also become a gorgeous pale pink, calling to mind cherry blossoms, making this a very springtimey soup – even more so because the Japanese word for glass noodles, *harusame*, means 'spring rain'.

Cut the radishes in half, then into half-circle slices about 3 mm (⅛ in) thick. Combine the radishes and dashi in a saucepan and bring to a high simmer. Cook for about 4 minutes until the radishes are translucent and slightly softened. Add the ponzu and noodles and continue to simmer for another 4 minutes until the noodles have plumped up and the radishes are cooked through. Taste, and add salt as needed. Garnish with the chives. Youcan serve this hot or chilled. It lasts for five days in the refrigerator.

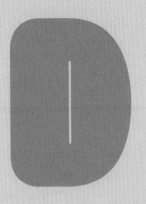

SMALL
SIDES

おかず

SMALL SIDES

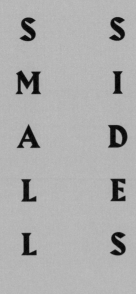

おかず

These recipes are called 'sides', but that's only because they are served alongside rice. The Japanese words for them would be *sōzai* or *okazu*, both of which literally translate quite plainly as 'vegetables'. And they are indeed often vegetables, but not always, just like they are not often really 'sides' – in some cases, they're really more like a main dish. It kind of depends on how many you decide to serve; serving yields are provided with a range, so if you are only preparing one or two of these, you'll end up on the lower end of those yields.

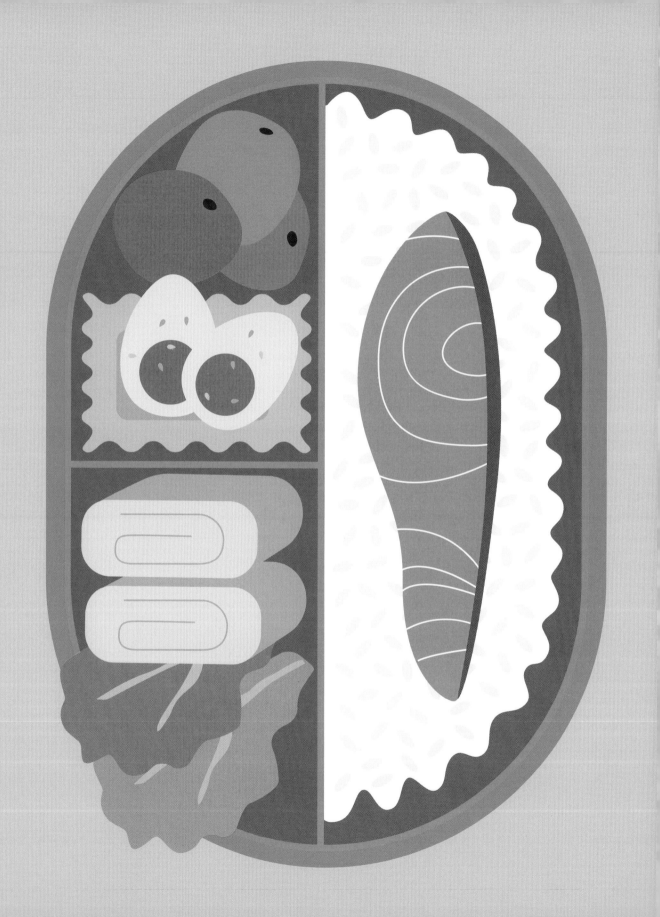

BENTO BASICS

BENTO BACKGROUND

In Japan, bento have many forms and fulfil many different roles. They range from ho-hum, grab-and-go lunches to grand, colourful arrangements of dishes artfully assembled and imbued with symbolism, as in the extravagant *osechi* bento prepared for New Year's celebrations. They can be cold or hot; homemade or shop-bought; wrapped in an elegant *furoshiki* or covered in cling film (plastic wrap); presented in beautiful lacquerware, or in flimsy plastic containers. My favourite subgenre of bento are *ekiben*: train station bento, which offer a taste of local produce even if you're just passing through, and often come in fanciful keepsake packaging. One such bento is packed into a box shaped like a warrior's face; one looks like a cow's head; another like a little train. There are some where the material itself expresses a more pre-modern vibe, such as bento made from woven bamboo, wood, wicker or earthenware. The now out-of-print *Ekiben* by Aki Tomura is an excellent reference that showcases the diversity of local bento in gorgeous, mouth-watering detail (but be warned, it contains no recipes).

What goes into a bento can be as varied as the containers themselves, incorporating the entirety of Japan's cuisines – if you can name it, it's probably been put into a bento somewhere. Is it fair to say that any Japanese food in a box is a bento? Sometimes I have trouble finding a way to reasonably refute this, but, still, intuitively I feel like the answer is no. Even at their most basic, there is an aesthetic sensibility to bento; they should have a certain balance to them, and ideally that balance should be included in the visual impact of the bento as well as the flavour.

Every single one of the books on bento I own mention colour – as do many of my other traditional Japanese cookbooks generally. In *Kamome*

Shokudo's Delicious Vegetable Bento, Ritsuko Funebashi writes, 'Consider a balance of colour, but if you can't be fussed, a few cherry tomatoes, or an umeboshi or some black sesame on the rice will make the bento look more delicious.' In *Bento Power*, Sara Kiyo Popowa goes into the importance of colour in more detail, explaining how even a simple bento ought to include the 'five colours' of traditional Japanese food: white, black, green, red and yellow.

This might sound like a lot, but it's actually pretty easy to achieve, bearing in mind that black can incorporate dark greens and browns, red can also include pink and purple and anything orange can also work for yellow. So, if you have a pretty basic bento with some rice (white), nori (black), omelette (yellow, pages 98–99) and cucumber and radish *sunomono* (green and red, page 116) then you're there already.

Of course, balance is key in terms of the food too, and that means incorporating a variety of textures, ingredients, nutrients and cooking methods. A bento of just rice and soy-seasoned mince (page 144) will be tasty, but unsatisfying. Add some steamed greens and some pickles and you'll have a much more rounded bento. The cleverness of the 'five colours' scheme is that if you incorporate those, chances are you'll be incorporating a wider variety of flavours and nutrients as well. In Makiko Itoh's essential *The Just Bento Cookbook*, she garnishes a delicious beef sukiyaki bento with blanched mangetout, and carrots and daikon cut into little stars and moons, cleverly brightening a sea of brown beef, and making the bento both more colourful and more nutritionally substantial. By the way, it may seem like a small thing, but getting veg cutters so you can fashion carrots into little hearts or beetroot into little flowers really does make bento more fun.

BISH BASH BENTO

How you actually pack a bento will depend on what you're putting in it, and what sort of bento you have. Here I will provide a guide for a sort of 'basic' bento – that is, a rectangular, single-tiered container – with a rice-based meal.

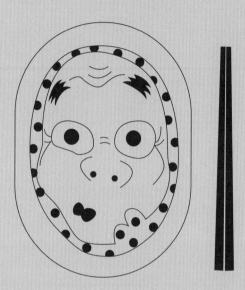

1
DECIDE WHETHER YOU ARE GOING TO HAVE YOUR BENTO HOT OR AT ROOM TEMPERATURE

This will determine what sort of bento you use as well as what you can put in it. Obviously, if you want to have something you're going to reheat in the microwave, you shouldn't use a stainless-steel bento and you shouldn't put nice, fresh salad leaves in it. (I do advise getting a tiered bento with two chambers, which will allow you to heat certain items separately while keeping others cold.) Hot bento should be packed with completely chilled food. For a room-temperature bento, just make sure nothing is hot when you pack it; excess steam has an adverse effect on both food quality and hygiene, so everything should be cool if not cold. But remember, rice that's been chilled in the refrigerator should be reheated before eating, otherwise it will be hard and chalky. If you don't plan to reheat your bento, pack it with freshly cooked (and cooled) rice – see page 28 for more details.

2
MAKE SURE YOUR BENTO IS CLEAN

This should really go without saying, but like... clean your bento, people! Some of them are dishwasher-safe, which is great, but others you'll have to wash by hand. Take particular care with wooden or bamboo bento, and be sure to dry them well after washing – although this is true for all bento. Most microbes simply can't survive in a dry environment, so always keep your bento free of water droplets and don't store them with the lids on, so they can air out.

3
PACK THE RICE IN

Typically, a rice-based bento will be about half-full of rice, with the rice pushed to one side of the container; this leaves room for one or two larger dishes, or three or four smaller ones, on the side. However, some dishes are intended to be eaten on top of rice, which are in category **F**. Consider this when adding the rice – do you want it off to one side, or as a bed underneath everything else? Or, in some cases, the entire bento may be rice, such as takikomi gohan (page 34) – in which case, fill 'er up and skip to step 5.

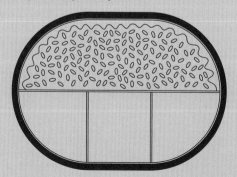

4
PACK THE SIDES IN

This is pretty straightforward – simply arrange your side dishes in a visually pleasing manner, taking into consideration how their flavours may mingle if they touch each other. You may wish to use little dividers to keep dishes separate, or create borders between items using sturdy salad leaves. A good bento should be tightly packed, so that things don't get jostled around in transit. It is also a good idea to pack sauces, condiments and salad dressings in separate pots – I reuse the little plastic ones I get with takeaways. Some things can be sauced or dressed ahead of time, but make sure nothing has too much excess liquid; pickles and similar items should be well drained.

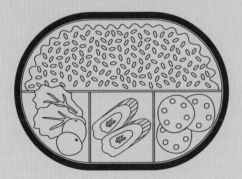

5
MAKE IT PRETTY

Remember the five colours – is there anything missing? A few sliced radishes, a little handful of pea shoots or some egg threads (page 97) can go a long way. To be honest, this is a bonus – but I do think part of the joy of bento is that it's like a present you get to unwrap for yourself at lunchtime. It is kind of a bummer if you open it up and it's just a big boxful of brown.

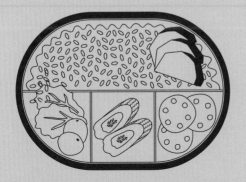

6
CONSIDER A SOUP

Soup is a great satisfier, and I often feel like lunch isn't quite complete without some. You have two options for bringing soup along with your bento: you can either pack it into a Thermos while still hot, or you can pack the stuff to make instant miso soup (page 75) and make it wherever you're eating, provided you have a kettle and a mug, cup or a bowl. On that note, it is also a good idea to bring your own cutlery (which can be whatever you fancy, though *waribashi*, or disposable chopsticks, are the preferred implement in Japan). Nothing is more disappointing than packing a delightful bento for yourself and then realising you have nothing to eat it with.

7
PACK IT UP AND GO!

Remember to make sure everything has cooled off before putting the lid on, then secure it with a band or clips or whatever your bento comes with. If you are concerned about leakages, well, first of all, you've packed your bento wrong, but if it is an ongoing problem, then simply invest in a leak-proof bento. You can also put your bento in a plastic bag as a precaution.

8
ENJOY

If you're reheating your bento, open the lid a crack to let the steam out, and microwave for a few minutes until nice and hot. If you're having your bento at room temperature, simply dive in, but bear in mind that bento are best eaten in the presence of other people, to make them jealous.

JAPANESE OMELETTE, THREE WAYS

AJITSUKE TAMAGO 味付け玉子

SERVES 2–4

4 eggs
1 tablespoon soy sauce
1 tablespoon sake
1 teaspoon sugar
pinch of salt
big pinch of dashi powder
1 teaspoon vegetable oil, or more as needed

Is Japan the greatest place in the world to eat eggs? I think it just might be. Consider all of the various preparations of eggs you can find in Japan: soft and wobbly onsen eggs, custardy *chawanmushi*, salty-fudgy marinated eggs for ramen, fluffy-creamy omelettes, creamy egg mayo sandwiches, tempura-fried eggs, panko-fried eggs, sukiyaki dipped in raw eggs, chicken-and-egg rice bowls ... I could go on, but my editor has put a pretty tight limit on my word count (my last book was longer than some novels).

So yes: lots of eggs. But the egg dish that may be most common is the humble *tamagoyaki*, or *dashimaki tamago*. Both refer to eggs that are beaten and seasoned (the latter with dashi), then fried in thin layers that are rolled up onto themselves like little carpets. This process is repeated until you end up with a chunky log of egg, which is then sliced to expose its concentric tree ring-like cross-sections. These are a staple of bento and breakfasts in particular, but they are also enjoyed for dinner.

The process of making *tamagoyaki* will take practise, but the practise itself will also teach you how to make a simpler type of Japanese omelette, called *usuyaki tamago*, which are essentially thin, crêpe-like sheets of egg. These are typically draped over rice or used to wrap around rice or other ingredients. They can also be stacked and sliced into little ribbons to make a third type of Japanese omelette preparation called *kinshi tamago*, a common rice topping that can be used as a garnish or in salads.

Beat all of the ingredients except the oil together well. If you want a really smooth, evenly coloured omelette, pass the mixture through a sieve before cooking. Ideally, the mixture should be in a little jug, which will make the cooking process easier.

You will need a good non-stick pan or well-seasoned cast-iron pan for this. For tamagoyaki, the process will be a lot easier and the end result much better in a rectangular Japanese egg pan, so if you plan on making this with any regularity, it's worth getting one. You can serve these omelettes at any temperature. They will last four days in the refrigerator.

FOR USUYAKI TAMAGO (EGG SHEETS) AND KINSHI TAMAGO (EGG THREADS):

Heat your pan over a medium heat and add the oil. Spread the oil around evenly with a folded-up sheet of paper towel. Pour in a little of the egg mixture – enough to cover the entire surface of the pan, but very thinly – about 2 mm (⅛ in) deep, maximum. Tilt the pan to make sure the egg is evenly spread, then leave to cook on one side for 2–3 minutes until the top of the egg is no longer wet. Carefully remove the sheet of cooked egg with a spatula or chopsticks and transfer to a cutting board. Repeat this process six or seven times until all the egg has been cooked. Keep an eye on the heat; ideally, the finished eggs should be bright yellow in colour, so keep browning to a minimum by maintaining a moderate, even heat.

To turn the egg sheets into egg threads, simply stack up the sheets and cut them into wide ribbons, about 4–5 cm (1½–2 in) wide. Cut across these ribbons to make thin threads, ideally no more than 2–3 mm (⅛ in) wide.

FOR DASHIMAKI TAMAGO (ROLLED OMELETTE):

Heat your pan over a medium heat and add the oil. Spread the oil around evenly with a folded-up sheet of paper towel. Pour in a little of the egg mixture – enough to cover the entire surface of the pan, but very thinly – about 2 mm (⅛ in) deep, maximum. Tilt the pan to make sure the egg is evenly spread, then leave to cook on one side for 1–2 minutes until the bottom of the egg is cooked, but the top is still slightly runny. Using a spatula or chopsticks, carefully roll the sheet of egg up onto itself like you're rolling a carpet. When you get to the end, use the spatula to press the egg against the side of the pan so it forms a tight roll.

Leaving the egg roll against the side of the pan, pour another small amount of egg mixture into the pan, tilting it again to cover the surface evenly. Use chopsticks or your spatula to gently lift up the rolled-up, cooked egg, so the raw egg mixture can get underneath it. Once the top of the newly poured egg sheet has almost set, roll the egg up once again, in the opposite direction, so you now have a thicker roll of egg. Repeat this process another 4–5 times, remembering to press the egg against the side of the pan after each completed roll, to make sure it sticks together.

Once all of the egg has been cooked, it can be sliced and eaten immediately, or kept for up to four days in the refrigerator.

MARINATED EGGS
AJITSUKE TAMAGO 味付け卵

MAKES 6 MARINATED EGGS

The quintessential ramen topping *ajitsuke tamago*, literally 'seasoned eggs', also makes excellent breakfast and bento fodder (not to mention a fabulous garnish for all sorts of other dishes). This recipe uses tsuyu as the pickling medium, which imparts the egg with moreish umami and a delicate smokiness without making it too salty. Store-bought tsuyu is good and very convenient, but also pretty expensive; you can make your own using the recipe on page 208. The addition of aromatic ingredients is partially inspired by Korean *mayak* eggs, which have recently become trendy in Japan.

Fill a large saucepan with water and bring it to a rolling boil, then lower in the eggs. Boil them for 6 minutes and 20 seconds, or 6 minutes and 40 seconds if you want the yolks more fudgy rather than gooey; cook for a full 7 minutes if you want your yolks quite firm (if you keep your eggs in the refrigerator, add 30 seconds to all of these timings). When the timer's up, remove the eggs with a slotted spoon, then chill them quickly in cold water. Stir together all the other ingredients. When they're completely cool, peel the eggs and soak them in the tsuyu mixture, in the refrigerator, for 4–24 hours. If you like, you can serve these with some of the marinade, as well as the spring onions and sesame spooned on top. Serve these cold or at room temperature. They last six days in the refrigerator.

6 large eggs, at room temperature
200 ml (7 fl oz/scant 1 cup) tsuyu
1 spring onion (scallion), finely sliced and rinsed under cold water
1 garlic clove, grated
1 cm (½ in) fresh ginger root, peeled and shredded
1 teaspoon sesame seeds
½ teaspoon vinegar
½ teaspoon sesame oil

ENOKI BACON ROLLS
ENOKI NO BĒKON MAKI えのきのベーコン巻き

SERVES 3–4

200 g (7 oz) enoki mushrooms
12 rashers of streaky bacon, unsmoked
black pepper, to taste
about 1 tablespoon cornflour (cornstarch)
1 tablespoon vegetable oil
1 tablespoon sake
1 tablespoon mirin
1 teaspoon soy sauce

Nikumaki is a Japanese preparation in which various ingredients, usually vegetables, are bundled up in strips of very thinly sliced meat, typically – but not always – pork belly. I've written previously about how I usually use bacon in place of the pork many Japanese recipes call for, and how in many cases, this is not only an adequate substitution but possibly even an upgrade. So, I decided to try it wrapped around enoki mushrooms, in the style of nikumaki. And it was indeed most satisfactory ... but then again, how could it not be?!

Cut about 2.5 cm (1 in) or so off the bottom of the enoki cluster and discard. Break the rest of the enoki into twelve little bundles. Wrap each of these bundles in a rasher of bacon, at an angle, so the bacon ends up covering almost the entire length of the enoki. Season each bundle well with black pepper, then dust them on all sides with cornflour, using a sieve to sprinkle it on. Heat the vegetable oil in a large frying pan (skillet) over a medium heat, then add the rolls. Fry for about 6–7 minutes until nicely browned on one side, then turn and repeat. Use a folded-up paper towel to carefully absorb any excess fat that has pooled in the pan. Combine the sake, mirin and soy sauce and pour over the rolls, then toss them to ensure they are evenly coated. When the liquid has reduced to a very thick, sticky glaze, remove from the heat and serve. You can serve these at any temperature. They will last for four days in the refrigerator.

SHOYU BUTTER SQUASH AND EDAMAME CROQUETTES

SHŌYU BATĀ AJI NO KABOCHA TO EDAMAME NO KOROKKE

醤油バター味のかぼちゃと枝豆のコロッケ

MAKES 8 CROQUETTES – SERVES 2–4

400 g (14 oz) squash or pumpkin
 (peeled weight), cut into large chunks
30 g (1 oz) butter, plus more for greasing
2 tablespoons soy sauce
½ tablespoon mirin
pinch of chilli powder (optional)
20–30 g (¾–1 oz) plain (all-purpose) flour,
 plus more, as needed
40 g (1½ oz) edamame beans
2 eggs, beaten with a splash of water or milk
50–60 g (2 oz) panko
vegetable oil, as needed
a few cos (romaine) lettuce leaves,
 shredded (optional)
lots and lots of tonkatsu sauce or ponzu

This recipe combines two all-time greats from Japanese cuisine: soy sauce butter and pumpkin croquettes. The combination of soy sauce and butter is so delicious that whoever invented it should have a holiday named after them, and pumpkin croquettes are brilliant because they're, you know, deep-fried pumpkin! Easy, tasty, versatile. Any squash will do for this, but if you can, choose a dense, sweet variety like kabocha or delica pumpkin.

Cook the squash by steaming, roasting or microwaving, but don't boil it or it will get waterlogged. My preference is roasting, as this heightens its flavour and sweetness. Do this at 200°C (400°F/gas 6) with a small amount of neutral oil for about 45 minutes until completely soft. While the squash is still hot, mash it with the butter, soy sauce, mirin and chilli (if using). For best results, use a blender or smash it through a sieve so it is nice and smooth. If your mixture is very wet and cannot be shaped into balls, stir in some plain flour until it thickens to the consistency of mashed potato. Stir the edamame into the mixture and leave to cool.

Line a baking sheet with baking parchment and grease your hands liberally with some butter. Grab blobs of the squash mixture and form it into eight balls, then lightly flatten these into patty shapes about 1 cm (½ in) deep. Place on the lined sheet, transfer to the refrigerator and leave to chill completely or they can be frozen, which will make them easier to pané.

Using your hands, carefully dredge each squash croquette in flour, then egg, then panko to ensure they are well coated in the breadcrumbs. Pour a 5 mm (¼ in) depth of oil into a wide, deep frying pan (skillet) and place over a high heat. Test the oil with some breadcrumbs; when they sizzle, lower the heat to medium-high and add the croquettes. Fry on each side for about 5 minutes until browned all over, and drain on paper towel. Serve on a mound of lettuce, if using, with plenty of tonkatsu sauce or ponzu on the side for dipping. This lasts four days in the refrigerator or one month in the freezer.

MICROWAVED PEA SHOOTS WITH GOMASHIO

KANTAN RENJI DE KANETSU TŌMYŌ NO GOMASHIO AE 簡単レンジで加熱豆苗のごま塩和え

SERVES 4

80–100 g (3–3½ oz) pea shoots
¼ teaspoon sugar
⅛ teaspoon MSG
1 teaspoon black sesame seeds
a few pinches of sea salt

I have no idea what prompted me to microwave pea shoots in the first place. Laziness, maybe? I love cooked pea shoots, but I don't love cleaning up frying pans or steamers. Anyway, I'm glad I tried this, because it is one of my very favourite vegetable okazu – fresh and sweet and crunchy and simple.

Combine the pea shoots, sugar and MSG in a microwave-safe container and toss. Loosely cover the container with a lid or cling film (plastic wrap) and microwave on high (700W) for 1 minute and 30 seconds. Decant into a serving dish and garnish with the sesame and salt. Serve at room temperature. This lasts four days in the refrigerator.

MICROWAVED RUNNER BEANS WITH YUZU GINGER MISO

RENJI DE KANETSU RANĀ BĪNZU NO SHŌGA YUZU MISO AE

レンジで加熱ラナービーンズの生姜柚子味噌和え

SERVES 4–8

Runner beans (and also green beans, which work well in this recipe) take on an interesting texture in the microwave. They remain crunchy but they also come out slightly desiccated, concentrating their flavour, which reminds me of the Chinese method of dry-frying, but without busting out the wok. The sauce in this recipe is one of those simple but fantastically delicious Japanese sauces that works well with just about anything – certainly any vegetable, but also most meats and seafood too.

Finely grate the ginger over a small bowl or container to catch its juice. Combine the grated ginger and juice with the miso, sugar, water and yuzu juice, and stir well with a fork or small whisk to combine, ensuring the sauce is quite smooth. Place the runner beans in a microwave-safe container. Loosely cover the container with a lid or cling film (plastic wrap) and microwave on high (700W) for 2 minutes, then toss the beans, re-cover, microwave for another 1 minute, then toss and cook for 1 more minute. To serve, spoon the sauce over each individual portion. (For bento, you can either toss the beans through the sauce or pack it in a small sauce pot.) Serve this at any temperature. It will keep for five days in the refrigerator.

1 cm (½ in) fresh ginger root, peeled
20 g (¾ oz) white miso
½ tablespoon sugar
½ tablespoon water
1 teaspoon yuzu juice (or similar citrus juice)
150–200 g (5–7 oz) runner beans (or similar green vegetable), de-stringed and cut into 1 cm pieces at an angle

MICROWAVED ASPARAGUS AND SPRING ONIONS WITH MUSTARD MISO VINEGAR SAUCE

RENJI DE KANETSU ASUPARA TO NEGI NO KARASHI SUMISO-AE

レンジで加熱アスパラとネギの辛子酢味噌和え

SERVES 4

4 tablespoons white miso
2 tablespoons sugar
2 tablespoons vinegar
¼ teaspoon English mustard
   or ½ teaspoon Dijon mustard
200–250 g (7–9 oz) asparagus, tough
   ends removed and discarded, cut into
   5 cm (2 in) chunks
4 spring onions (scallions), cut into 5 cm
   (2 in) chunks
a few pinches of sesame seeds

Accentuate the freshness of beautiful springtime produce at its peak by cooking it in the best way possible: in the microwave. Seriously though, because of how microwaves steam ingredients using their own moisture, they're fantastic at preserving colour, texture and flavour – ideal for sweet, seasonal green veg like asparagus and spring onions. The sauce for this dish, called *sumiso* (vinegared miso), has a nice balance of acidity and richness and is seasoned with a little strong mustard; it is very versatile and tastes great either hot or cold.

To make the sauce, stir together the miso, sugar, vinegar and mustard until smooth. Place the asparagus and spring onions in a microwave-safe container. Loosely cover the container with a lid or cling film (plastic wrap) and microwave on high (700W) for 2½ minutes. To serve, spoon the sauce over individual portions. (For bento, you can either toss the veg through the sauce or put it in a pot on the side.) Garnish with the sesame and serve at any temperature.

   The vegetables will last about five days in the refrigerator, but they are better within three; the sauce will keep for up to a year.

MICROWAVED MABO AUBERGINE

RENJI DE KANETSU MĀBŌ NASU レンジで加熱麻婆茄子

SERVES 4, OR ENOUGH FOR UP TO **8** BENTO

1 aubergine (eggplant),
    quartered lengthways
1 cm (½ in) fresh ginger root, peeled
    and finely shredded
2 garlic cloves, roughly chopped
1 tablespoon brown sugar
2 tablespoons doubanjiang or gochujang
2 tablespoons water
2 teaspoons cornflour (cornstarch)
1 tablespoon sake
1 tablespoon red miso
1 teaspoon ketchup
1 teaspoon vinegar
¼ teaspoon MSG
¼ teaspoon sanshō pepper or finely
    ground Sichuan pepper (optional)
100 g (3½ oz) minced (ground) pork
    or beef (or vegan equivalent)
½ green (bell) pepper, roughly chopped
5 cm (2 in) piece of leek, halved and cut
    into 5 mm (¼ in) slices
1 tablespoon oil
1 teaspoon sesame oil or chilli oil
soy sauce, to taste
chilli (hot pepper) flakes, to garnish

Mābō nasu is a popular Japanese variation on the classic Sichuanese *mapo tofu*. I love it because aubergine has a similar squishy texture to silken tofu, but it absorbs the sauce better. The only problem is that aubergine typically requires a *lot* of oil to cook properly, which is not ideal for a bento. Enter our old friend, the microwave. Because microwaves steam vegetables using the moisture already within them, aubergines become soft and fudgy from the inside out, without getting waterlogged, when you cook them this way. And of course, this method can't be beat for convenience – you can even store the finished dish in the same container you cook it in.

Wrap each quarter of aubergine individually in cling film (plastic wrap), then microwave on high (700W) for 2–3 minutes until softened but not yet cooked through. Set aside to cool while you prepare the sauce. Combine the ginger, garlic, sugar, doubanjiang, water, cornflour, sake, miso, ketchup, vinegar, MSG and sanshō and mix well so no lumps of miso remain. When the aubergine is cool enough to handle, unwrap it and cut it into 2 cm (¾ in) chunks. Place the meat in a microwave-safe container and cover loosely with a lid or cling film (plastic wrap). Microwave on high (700W) for 2 minutes, then break up the mince with a fork. Add the prepared aubergine, pepper, leek and the oils and mix well, then re-cover the container and microwave again for another 4 minutes. Pour in the sauce, mix well, re-cover and microwave for 4 minutes. Check that the aubergine is cooked through by piercing it with a chopstick or cutting it with a spoon – it should be completely soft. Taste, and adjust seasoning as needed with soy sauce. Decant into a serving dish, garnish with chilli flakes and serve hot or at room temperature. This lasts five days in the refrigerator.

SMALL SIDES

CUCUMBER AND RADISH VINEGARED SALAD

KYŪRI TO RADISSHU NO SUNOMONO きゅうりとラディッシュの酢の物

SERVES 8

1 cucumber, halved and de-seeded
200 g (7 oz) radishes
salt, as needed
3 tablespoons vinegar
2 tablespoons sugar
1 tablespoon soy sauce
sesame seeds, to garnish

Sunomono are salads that border on pickle territory – they literally translate as 'vinegared things'. Perhaps the most common variety is made with cucumber and wakame, but another popular option are small turnips called *kabu*. This recipe sort of combines the two, with radishes instead of turnips, providing a colourful contrast to the cucumbers.

Slice the cucumber and radishes as thinly as you can; use a mandoline if you have one. Salt them very liberally – use handfuls rather than pinches of salt. Massage the salt into the veg and leave them for 30 minutes. Meanwhile, stir together the vinegar, sugar and soy sauce until the sugar dissolves. Rinse the vegetables well, then squeeze them very firmly to extract as much excess water as possible. Stir through the dressing, and keep in the refrigerator until ready to serve. Garnish each portion with a pinch of sesame and serve cold. This lasts five days in the refrigerator.

KINPIRA BEETROOT

KINPIRA BĪTSU きんぴらビーツ

SERVES 4

1 tablespoon sesame oil
250 g (9 oz) raw beetroot (beet),
    peeled and julienned
3 tablespoons soy sauce
1 tablespoon mirin
1 tablespoon light brown sugar
¼ teaspoon dashi powder
pinch of chilli (hot pepper) flakes
1 tablespoon sesame seeds

One of the most common vegetable sides to find in bento is *kinpira*, dish of sautéed vegetables in a sweet, sticky, slightly spicy sauce characterised by a generous dose of sesame oil. Perhaps the most popular kinpira item is burdock, which has a delicious earthiness and crunchy texture. It's not the easiest vegetable to find, but I've found that beetroot makes an excellent substitute, with a similar earthy flavour and toothsomeness.

Heat the sesame oil in a frying pan (skillet) over a medium heat and add the beetroot. Sauté for about 10 minutes, stirring or tossing frequently until lightly browned. Add all the seasonings except the sesame, and continue to sauté until the liquid has reduced to a sticky glaze and the beetroot has become tender (but still al dente). Stir in the sesame, then remove from the heat. This can be served hot but it is equally good, if not better, cold. This lasts five days in the refrigerator.

SPICY AVOCADO AND TOFU SALAD

ABOKADO TO TŌFU NO PIRIKARA POKĪ FU アボカドと豆腐のピリ辛ポキー風

SERVES 2 OR MAKES ENOUGH FOR UP TO 4 BENTO

A while ago I had some tuna *yukke* (spicy Korean-style tartare) that my friend Fumio made. The tuna was tasty, of course, but what I really loved about it was the deliciously spicy gochujang sauce and the fresh, creamy garnish of chopped avocado with lime. I've combined both in this recipe, and used tofu as the protein, because actually the seasonings here work very well with its cheesy blandness. Feel free to use actual raw tuna if you like but, if you do, be sure to eat it fresh or keep it cold at all times, especially if you're taking it in a bento.

Cut the tofu into 1 cm (½ in) slices and microwave for 1 minute to expel excess moisture. Drain and pat dry with paper towel, then leave to cool while you prepare the rest of the dish. Stir together all of the seasonings until smooth and well mixed. When the tofu is cool, cut it into 1 cm (½ in) dice, then stir together with the dressing and the avocado. Garnish each portion with a pinch of sesame and serve. This lasts two days in the refrigerator.

180 g (6⅓ oz) firm cotton (block) tofu
1½ tablespoons gochujang
1 tablespoon soy sauce
1 tablespoon mayonnaise
juice of ½ lime (about 1 tablespoon)
½ teaspoon vinegar
½ teaspoon sugar
½ teaspoon sesame oil
½ garlic clove, finely grated
1 avocado, diced
sesame seeds, to garnish

CELERIAC AND CHIVE SHIRA-AE

SERORIAKKU TO KONEGI NO SHIRA-AE セロリアックと小ねぎの白和え

SERVES 4 OR MAKES ENOUGH FOR UP TO 8 BENTO

½ celeriac, peeled
1 carrot, peeled
5–6 radishes
salt, as needed
150 g (5 oz) firm or extra-firm
    silken tofu
2 tablespoons white miso
2 tablespoons sesame seeds, ground
    to the consistency of coarse sand
2 tablespoons soy sauce
1 tablespoon mirin
1 teaspoon lemon juice
¼ teaspoon dashi powder
10 g (½ oz) chives, roughly chopped

Shira-ae is a style of Japanese salad that uses mashed tofu to create a creamy yet light dressing. It works with pretty much everything, but I like it with celeriac, calling to mind a classic remoulade. I like shira-ae to be super smooth and creamy, so I use a blender, but traditionally the tofu is a bit coarser, mashed in a mortar, so feel free to do it that way if you prefer a bit more texture.

Finely slice the vegetables, about 2 mm (⅛ in) thick – use a mandoline if you have one. Julienne the celeriac and carrot, then combine with the radishes in a bowl. Sprinkle with a generous amount of salt, then massage this into the veg and leave to tenderise for about 20 minutes. Meanwhile, make the dressing by combining the tofu, miso, sesame, soy sauce, mirin, lemon juice and dashi and blending until smooth. Rinse the salt off of the vegetables and squeeze them dry, then toss through the dressing along with the chives. This lasts up to five days in the refrigerator, but is best eaten within three.

THE CAULIFLOWER THAT TRIED AND FAILED TO BE KARAAGE, AKA 'WHY CAN'T I STOP EATING THIS?' CAULIFLOWER

KARAAGE NI NARITAKATTA KARIFURAWĀ 唐揚げになりたかったカリフラワー

SERVES 2–4

1 garlic clove, finely grated
1–2 cm (½–¾ in) fresh ginger root, finely grated
2 tablespoons oil, plus a little more, for greasing
1 tablespoon sake
1 tablespoon mirin
1 tablespoon soy sauce
1 teaspoon sesame oil
¼ teaspoon salt
⅛ teaspoon MSG or dashi powder
big pinch of white pepper
20 g (¾ oz/⅛ cup) cornflour (cornstarch)
400 g (14 oz) cauliflower florets, or one medium head of cauliflower

In any creative project, it's important to set rules to keep you focused and in line with your overall mission. For this book, I have a few rules too, and one of them is no deep-frying. This is not easy, because deep-frying is an important part of Japanese cookery, and it's delicious. But this book is all about minimising faff – and while deep-frying isn't difficult, it's kind of annoying to set up and to clean up after. So, I wanted to try a cauliflower karaage recipe that could be roasted or shallow-fried instead of deep-fried, and let me tell you ... it did not work. At all. And I might have broken my rule against deep-frying if it weren't for the fact that the roasted version of this was still really, *really* delicious – a testament, I suppose, to how tasty a classic karaage marinade is. Besides, this recipe, like most of the ones in this book, is meant to work in a bento – and although karaage and other deep-fried items do commonly feature in bento, they never really remain crisp – so there's little point to deep-frying them in the first place.

You may rightfully be sceptical of this recipe, because it breaks a couple of rules itself, namely *don't substitute chicken for cauliflower* and *don't bake stuff that ought to be deep-fried*. But honestly, the results speak for themselves: addictively salty, umami nuggets of caramelised cauliflower in a flavour-packed marinade, with minimal effort and washing up. Even my avowedly anti-vegetable four-year-old cannot stop eating these.

Cut the cauliflower into florets that are larger than bite-size but no bigger than about 5 cm (2 in) across at their widest point. Whisk together all of the ingredients except the cauliflower until well-mixed and smooth. Toss the cauliflower, gently but thoroughly, through the marinade, ensuring it is very well coated – it's best to use your hands for this.

Preheat a fan oven to 200°C (400°F/gas 6) and lightly oil a baking sheet. Toss the cauliflower once again before spreading it out in a single layer on the sheet, spaced out from each other. Roast for 25 minutes, turning the cauliflower frequently, then turn the oven up to 240°C (475°F/gas 9) and roast for another 10 minutes, again turning once or twice during cooking to ensure even colouring. Transfer to a dish or tray lined with paper towel to blot away any excess oil before serving. Like actual karaage, this really does not need a dip, but you could have it with mayonnaise or ponzu if you like. You can keep the cauliflower in the marinade in the refrigerator for up to a day before cooking and for five days after cooking.

SALTED SALMON

SAKE NO SHIOYAKI 鮭の塩焼き

SERVES 4–8

200–250 g (7–9 oz) salmon, pin-boned
 and scaled
salt, as needed

Salted fish, especially oily fish, is a stalwart staple of any Japanese meal. Liberally salting and partially drying fish has several advantages: it seasons the fish (duh), firms its flesh, tenderises its skin, improves its colour and extends its refrigerator life by a day or two. Fish is sold pre-salted in Japan, but it's very, very easy to do at home, provided you have time, and room in the refrigerator. You can apply this method to any oily fish by the way – trout, mackerel, sardines and even tuna all work. You will need a tray with a wire rack for this recipe.

Cut the salmon into thin fillets – not much thicker than 1 cm (½ in) thick. Salt the fish on all sides liberally, not like you're trying to cure it, but perhaps twice as much salt than you would use just to season it normally. Gently rub the salt into the fish to ensure it is evenly distributed, then lay on a wire rack on a tray and leave uncovered in the refrigerator for at least 24 hours – two days is better. At this point, you can transfer the salted fillets to a container and they will keep in the refrigerator for another 2–3 days, or transfer to the freezer and they will last more than a month. If you freeze them, pack them in between sheets of parchment, so that individual portions can be easily retrieved.

Salted salmon can be cooked any way you would cook salmon normally, but I think it is best cooked under a very, very hot grill (broiler) until lightly charred. You can also cook it directly from frozen. Once cooked, you can serve it at any temperature. It will last for up to four days in the refrigerator.

MISO-MAPLE SALMON

SAKE NO MĒPURU MISOZUKE 鮭のメープル味噌漬け

SERVES 4–8

Japan's ongoing love affair with pancakes – which range from humdrum convenience store hotcakes to elaborate towers of cloud-like cakes made by fiercely whipping the batter like a meringue – means that maple syrup is no longer an exotic ingredient there. It isn't used so often in savoury dishes, but it tastes amazing when combined with miso as a marinade for salmon – a combination I was introduced to by my good friend and former head chef, Rivaaj Maharaj. The maple balances the saltiness and tang of the miso beautifully, and helps the fish develop a gorgeous char under the grill while also firming its texture.

Stir together the miso and the maple syrup until well-mixed, with no lumps of miso. Cut the salmon into four thin fillets, and rub them all over with the maple-miso mixture. Pack into a container and marinate overnight and for up to three days – the longer you leave them, the more delicious they will be. At this point, you can also transfer them to the freezer and they will last more than a month. If you freeze them, pack each fillet in between sheets of parchment, so that individual portions can be easily retrieved. Cook from chilled or frozen under a hot grill (broiler) until lightly charred. Serve at any temperature once cooked or refrigerate and eat within four days.

40 g (1½ oz) red miso
1½ tablespoons maple syrup
200–250 g (7–9 oz) salmon, pin-boned
and scaled

MACKEREL SIMMERED WITH ONIONS AND GINGER

SABA TO TAMANEGI NO NITSUKE 鯖と玉ねぎの煮付け

SERVES **4–8**

4 mackerel fillets
(350–400 g/12–14 oz), boned
1 medium onion, finely sliced
2 cm (¾ in) fresh ginger root,
peeled and finely shredded
150 ml (5 fl oz/scant ⅔ cup) sake
6 tablespoons mirin
4 tablespoons light brown sugar
4 tablespoons soy sauce

This recipe is a hybrid of two other recipes from the Japanese recipe resources I use the most: Shizuo Tsuji's seminal *Japanese Cooking: A Simple Art*, and the Japanese recipe site and magazine *Orange Page*. These two texts are very, very different. The former is an extremely thorough and detailed volume of classical dishes and techniques that captures the refined beauty of traditional Japanese cuisine; the latter also focuses on simple recipes and techniques, but it skews more modern and silly. Browsing it today, I came across a KFC copycat recipe and one for something called 'carbonara *mochi*'. Hell yes.

It delights me when I find commonalities between *Orange Page* and *A Simple Art*, because it illustrates an important through-line in Japanese cuisine, which is that good food really can be simple, unpretentious and accessible. *Orange Page*'s recipe for mackerel simmered with onions, for example, is very similar to Tsuji's classic sake-simmered mackerel. Dishes like these are timeless because they're not only delicious, but the kind of thing just about anybody can work into their daily repertoire.

Score the mackerel skin and cut each fillet in half to make eight pieces in total. Cut a circle of baking parchment to fit just inside a wide saucepan or deep frying pan (skillet). Combine the onion, ginger and sake in that pan and bring to a high simmer. Cook for about 3 minutes so the ginger infuses and the onion begins to soften, then lay the mackerel pieces in the pan, skin side up, in a single layer, and add the mirin, sugar and as much water as you need to come up to the surface of the mackerel (but not submerge it). Bring to the boil, then add the soy sauce and cover with the parchment – it should rest directly on the mackerel. Leave to boil for 10 minutes. To serve, place the mackerel skin-side up in dishes with some onions and ginger on top, and a spoonful of the sauce poured over. This will keep for up to five days in the refrigerator and can be enjoyed cold, but it will become saltier over time. Serve at any temperature, but to reheat, it is best to remove the mackerel from the sauce and grill (broil) it until lightly coloured and warm throughout.

PRAWN COCKTAIL WITH 'OKONOMIYAKI' DIP

SHURINPU KAKUTERU TO OKONOMIYAKI AJI DIP シュリンプカクテルとお好み焼き味ディップ

SERVES 2–4

Over dinner the other day, my wife and I were discussing our 'desert island' condiments: the table sauces and seasonings we just couldn't live without. Chilli oil and ketchup were mentioned. I considered furikake. Ponzu came to mind. But the two we agreed upon without hesitation were Kewpie mayo and Japanese brown sauce (specifically tonkatsu sauce or okonomiyaki sauce). Together, they can make pretty much everything taste delicious, but I think they're especially good with white meat and shellfish; combined with a few other seasonings, they make a perfect dip for chilled prawns.

If your prawns are frozen, defrost them, drain them well and pat them dry with a clean cloth or paper towel. If they haven't already been deveined, you can cut through the back of the shell with a sharp knife and remove the vein while keeping the shell on. Grill (broil) the prawns for about 6 minutes on high until they are cooked through, and their shells have coloured slightly. If the prawns have their heads on, remove the heads and reserve. Squeeze the goo from the head into a small bowl or ramekin (as that's where the richest, prawniest flavour is), then stir in the mayonnaise, brown sauce, ketchup, pickled ginger, wasabi and dashi powder. To serve, lay the prawns on top of the lettuce, put the sauce in a little dip pot (with a lid if it's going in a bento) and garnish the prawns with the chives, sesame and aonori. This lasts three days in the refrigerator.

200 g (7 oz) very large raw prawns (shrimp), shell on and deveined
2 tablespoons Kewpie mayonnaise
1 tablespoon okonomiyaki sauce or tonkatsu sauce
1 tablespoon ketchup
10 g (⅓ oz) pickled ginger, very finely chopped
½ teaspoon wasabi
⅛ teaspoon dashi powder
a few little gem lettuce leaves
a few chives, finely chopped
big pinch of sesame seeds
pinch of aonori flakes

GRILLED VEGETABLE SALAD WITH 'GENGHIS KHAN' DRESSING

JINGISUKAN FŪMI YAKI YASAI SARADA ジンギスカン風味焼き野菜サラダ

SERVES **4–8**

For the Sauce

4 tablespoons soy sauce
3 tablespoons beer (nothing too bitter)
½ eating apple, peeled and cored
1 small garlic clove
1.5 cm (⅔ in) fresh ginger root,
    peeled and finely sliced
1½ tablespoons mirin
1½ tablespoons honey or maple syrup
1 tablespoon light brown sugar
1 tablespoon vinegar
juice of ½ lemon
1 tablespoon sesame seeds
2 teaspoons sesame oil
¼ teaspoon pepper
pinch of chilli powder or shichimi pepper

For the Salad

1 medium onion, halved and finely sliced
about 300 g (10½ oz) squash, peeled
    and cut into little batons or wedges
    no thicker than 1 cm (½ in)
200 g (7 oz) bean sprouts
½ sweetheart (hispi) cabbage or
    ¼ ordinary cabbage, roughly chopped
1 (bell) pepper, cut into 1 cm (½ in) strips
1 tablespoon oil
salt, as needed

This recipe is inspired by the iconic Hokkaido beer hall speciality known as 'Genghis Khan', a simple but effective dish of barbecued lamb and vegetables served with a fruity and mouth-wateringly tangy sauce. While it may have one of the most dubious names in all of Japanese gastronomy– it has little, if anything, to do with actual Mongolian cuisine – it is also one of the most delicious, and that's as much due to the grilled veg and sauce as it is to do with the lamb. This recipe uses them on their own for a tasty, substantial salad that can be enjoyed at any temperature.

By the way, you may find the list of ingredients for the sauce a bit daunting, but it is still very easy to make. If it feels like a bit of a faff, make more of it and use it for other dishes – like many of the sauces in this book, it's very, very versatile, and will work well with all kinds of meat and protein as well as veg.

To make the sauce, blend everything together until quite smooth – the sesame should be broken down well, which will help thicken and emulsify the sauce. Set a rack in the oven about 10–12 cm (4–5 in) below the grill (broiler), and preheat the oven to as high as it will go (for me, this is 250°C/500°F/ gas 10), with the grill on high as well. Toss the prepared veg with the oil and a generous pinch of salt, then lay out in a shallow layer on a baking tray (pan). Roast/grill the veg for 15–20 minutes, turning them two or three times during cooking until cooked through and lightly blackened. Toss through the dressing while still warm and, if you can, leave to sit in the sauce for a while before serving (unusually for a salad, this one is best after a few days). Toss again before eating. Serve at any temperature, but it lasts five days in the refrigerator (the sauce will last longer if kept separately).

RAMEN TOPPINGS SALAD WITH ROASTED GARLIC SESAME DRESSING

RAMEN GU NO SARADA ラーメン具のサラダ

SERVES **4–6**

I used to think that the most important thing in a bowl of ramen is the broth, and I get the impression that this is what a lot of people think. There is some truth to this; the broth, in conjunction with the seasoning, is what flavours and characterises the entire bowl, so it *is* very important, don't get me wrong. But the elements of ramen are an ensemble cast; there is no one star of the show. My ramen epiphany came when eating a bowl of *tonkotsu* ramen at Daikokuya in Los Angeles; while the broth was what initially captured my attention, it was the interaction of all the different elements that kept me enraptured to the very last slurp. A lot of this had to do with the toppings – the way they got caught up in the noodles and provided little bursts of flavour and texture. The crunch of bean sprouts, the tang of pickled ginger and bamboo shoots, the freshness of spring onions – they may not be the things that ramen devotees obsess over, but the broth and noodles would be forlorn without them. This salad is a tribute to the unsung heroes of ramen, in all their crunchy, fresh, pickley glory.

To make the dressing, heat the sesame oil in a small saucepan over a medium-low heat and add the garlic. Slowly pan-roast them, tossing occasionally, for about 12 minutes until they are richly coloured on the outside and soft throughout. Remove from the heat and leave to cool. Blitz the sesame to a coarse sand consistency in a food processor, then add the garlic and oil from the pan (use a spatula to make sure you get all of it) and all the other ingredients. Purée until a rough dressing forms. Toss the dressing through the prepared vegetables just before serving. (If you are eating this later, the salt from the bamboo and pickled ginger will draw liquid from the other ingredients, so drain this liquid off before adding the dressing.) Serve at any temperature. It lasts for three days in the refrigerator.

For the Dressing

1 tablespoon sesame oil
5 garlic cloves, peeled and crushed
   with the side of a knife
2 tablespoons sesame seeds
20 g (¾ oz) tahini
20 g (¾ oz) white miso
20 g (¾ oz) caster (superfine) sugar
2 tablespoons water
1 tablespoon rice vinegar
1 tablespoon soy sauce
2 teaspoons lemon juice

For the Salad

150 g (5 oz) bean sprouts, blanched
   or microwaved and drained well
½ sweetheart (hispi) cabbage, cut into
   roughly 5 mm (¼ in) wide strips
2 spring onions (scallions), very finely
   sliced at an angle
50 g (2 oz) bamboo shoots, ideally
   menma, julienned, rinsed and drained
30 g (1 oz) red pickled ginger
½ batch of eggs threads
   (page 97, optional)

LACQUERED SPAM

TERIYAKI PŌKU 照焼きポーク

SERVES 2-8

1 tin (340 g/12 oz) Spam
2 tablespoons honey
1 tablespoon sake
1 tablespoon soy sauce
1 teaspoon ketchup
½ teaspoon gochujang or similar
    chilli paste
½ teaspoon sesame oil
½ teaspoon vinegar
vegetable oil, as needed
2 sheets of nori, cut into 8 long
    strips (optional)

Spam is a tricky one. On the one hand, I love it, and it is a legitimate part of Japanese gastronomy – specifically in Okinawa, and among the Japanese diaspora of Hawaii. On the other hand, it's ethically and nutritionally questionable (to say the least), and it only came to be adopted into Japanese cooking via the American military-industrial complex. Is Spam a delicious, convenient, perfectly legitimate and beloved Japanese ingredient, or is it just a salty, fatty, unpleasant pink lump of colonial jetsam? Could it be both? F. Scott Fitzgerald said, 'The test of a first-rate intelligence is the ability to hold two opposing ideas in mind at the same time and still retain the ability to function.'

You look like you're of first-rate intelligence. Here's a Spam recipe!

Cut the Spam into eight slices. Stir together all the remaining ingredients, except the vegetable oil and nori, until everything is smooth and well-mixed. Heat a little vegetable oil over a medium-high heat in a large frying pan (skillet), then use a paper towel to evenly coat the pan with oil and mop up any excess. Fry the Spam on each side for about 4 minutes until nicely browned, then pour in the sauce. Stir-fry for another 3–4 minutes until the liquid has reduced and caramelised and formed a sticky glaze that clings to the Spam.

These can be served alongside rice or on top of it, or better yet, as *musubi* – pack some rice into the empty Spam container to mould it into Spam-shaped bricks of rice, then place the cooked Spam on top of it and wrap each one in nori. Serve this at any temperature. It lasts for five days in the refrigerator.

3

BIG SIDES
メインディッシュ

F

RICE BOWL TOPPINGS

丼の具

G

ONE-DISH DINNERS

ワンプレート夕食

BIG SIDES

RICE BOWL

TOPPING

ONE-DISH

DINNERS

丼の具

メインディッシュ

ワンプレート夕食

These dishes are a bit more substantial than those found in the previous chapter, but generally occupy the same role – they're things to have with rice but, in this case, they go on top rather than on the side. This makes for some hearty donburi, although this chapter also includes noodle dishes.

SOBORO (SOY-SEASONED MINCE)
SOBORO そぼろ

SERVES 4

1 tablespoon oil
500 g (1 lb 2 oz) minced (ground) meat
of your choice – chicken is classic,
but you can also use turkey, beef,
pork, lamb, crumbled tofu or any
plant-based equivalent
2.5 cm (1 in) fresh ginger root, peeled and
grated (including the juice that comes
from grating)
3 tablespoons soy sauce
1 tablespoon sake
1 tablespoon sugar
1 tablespoon mirin
1 teaspoon sesame seeds

Soboro is a classic rice bowl or bento topping with one
of the highest simplicity-to-satisfaction ratios I know of.
Essentially stir-fried minced meat (usually chicken) highly
seasoned with ginger and soy sauce, it acts as both a hearty
protein and an effective seasoning for rice. (You can even
dehydrate it to make a very delicious furikake.)

Heat the oil over a high heat in a large frying pan (skillet) and
add the mince, breaking it up into crumbles with a spatula.
Once the mince has mostly cooked through, leave it to brown
for about 5 minutes. Add the ginger and its juice along with
the other ingredients, except the sesame, then continue
to stir-fry until the liquid has reduced to almost nothing and
has been absorbed into the meat. Remove from the heat
and stir in the sesame. You can serve this hot or at room
temperature. It lasts for five days in the refrigerator or two
months in the freezer.

TOFU AND VEGETABLES IN SWEET RED MISO 'CHAJAN' SAUCE

TŌFU TO YASAI NO CHAJAN SŌSU AE 豆腐と野菜のチャジャンソース和え

MAKES 4 BABY BEAR SERVINGS, 3 MAMA BEAR SERVINGS OR 2 PAPA BEAR SERVINGS

This one is basically an attempt to recreate a Korean sauce based on a pungent fermented black bean paste called *chunjang*, but using Japanese ingredients. In Korea, this sauce is usually served on noodles, in a classic dish called *jjajangmyeon*, which in Japan is known as *chajanmyon* – not to be confused with the similar Sino-Japanese dish *jājāmen*, or the northern Chinese original, *zhajiangmian*, which is flavoured primarily with a sweet bean paste called *tianmianjiang*. In Japan, a common substitute for tianmianjiang (or *tenmenjan*, in Japanese) is very dark red miso, such as Hatchō miso, which is what I've used here.

So, this is essentially a sweet, rich and tangy chajanmyon-style sauce, which is based on jjajangmyeon and related to zhajiangmian or jājāmen, but which does not use chunjang or tianmianjiang (a.k.a. tenmenjan). You follow? Good! Let's cook.

Pour the boiled water over the dried mushrooms and leave to soak for at least 15 minutes. Meanwhile, cut all of the vegetables into a 1 cm (½ in) dice (you can just quarter the radishes). Stir together the miso, garlic, soy sauce, sake and Worcestershire sauce to make a paste with no lumps of miso. When the mushrooms have rehydrated, squeeze them dry (retain the liquid), discard their stems and cut the caps into strips about 5 mm (¼ in) wide.

Heat the oil in a frying pan (skillet) over a medium heat and add the onions, carrots and radishes. Stir-fry for about 6 minutes until everything has softened slightly and begun to colour. Add the sweet potato and mushrooms and stir-fry for another 4–5 minutes until the sweet potato has taken on some colour as well. Add the miso mixture, then stir-fry well for 2–3 minutes, so the miso coats the vegetables well and caramelises slightly. Stir together the cornflour and cold water to make a thin slurry, then add this to the pan along with the mushroom liquid, sugar, sesame oil and butter, if using. Stir well and let everything come to the boil, then keep at a high simmer for about 6–7 minutes until all of the veg are nice and tender. Add the peas and pepper and stir them through, then gently add the tofu and shake the pan to coat the tofu in the sauce. If you're using noodles, cook them according to the package instructions, rinse them briefly under running water, drain well, then transfer to shallow bowls. Serve the tofu on top of the noodles, or on top or to the side of cooked rice. Garnish with the spring onions or chives and eat while hot. This lasts for five days in the refrigerator if you keep the rice or noodles separate.

100 ml (3½ fl oz/scant ½ cup) just-boiled water
8 (10–15 g/½ oz) dried shiitake mushrooms
100 g (3½ oz) radishes
180 g (6⅓ oz) (1 smallish) sweet potato, peeled
1 small onion
1 carrot, peeled
60 g (2 oz) dark red miso – use the darkest miso you can find, such as Hatchō miso or a brown rice miso
2–3 garlic cloves, finely grated
3 tablespoons soy sauce
2 tablespoons sake
1 tablespoon Worcestershire sauce
2 tablespoons oil
1 tablespoon cornflour (cornstarch)
150 ml (5 fl oz/scant ⅔ cup) cold water
2½ tablespoons dark brown sugar
½ teaspoon sesame oil
10 g (½ oz) butter (optional)
40 g (1½ oz) peas
lots of freshly ground pepper
300 g (10½ oz) extra firm silken tofu, cut into roughly 2 cm (¾ in) cubes
2 spring onions (scallions) or handful of chives, finely sliced
3–4 portions of noodles or cooked rice

GYOZA-FILLING RICE BOWL

GYOZA NO TANE DONBURI 餃子のタネ丼

SERVES 2–4

1 tablespoon oil
200 g (7 oz) fatty minced (ground) pork
6 leaves of Chinese leaf (napa cabbage),
    cut into 1 cm (½ in) pieces
4 garlic cloves, minced or finely grated
15 g (½ oz) fresh ginger root, peeled
    and very finely chopped
1 teaspoon sesame oil
2 tablespoons soy sauce
2 tablespoons sake
1 tablespoon cornflour (cornstarch)
1 teaspoon rice vinegar or lemon juice
salt, MSG and white pepper, to taste
2 portions cooked rice
2 egg yolks
2 spring onions (scallions), finely sliced
1 teaspoon sesame seeds
1 teaspoon chilli oil (optional)

Lately, I've come across several recipes for what are sometimes fancifully called 'wrapper-less gyoza rice bowls', i.e. stir-fried gyoza filling on rice, i.e. something for people who want to eat gyoza but don't have any frozen gyoza in the house and can't be arsed to make them. Frankly, this is ingenious – it's about as quick and easy as soboro (page 144) and, of course, it does taste like gyoza, but you can eat it with a spoon. Magnificent!

Heat the oil in a frying pan (skillet) over a high heat. Add the pork mince, Chinese leaf, garlic and ginger and stir-fry for about 8 minutes until the pork is lightly browned. Stir together the sesame oil, soy sauce, sake, cornflour and vinegar, then pour this into the mince mixture. Let it boil for a few minutes, then taste and adjust the seasoning with salt, MSG and lots of white pepper. Scoop the pork onto piles of rice in deep bowls and place the egg yolks on top of each one. Garnish with the spring onions and sesame, drizzle over the chilli oil, if using, and serve hot. This lasts four days in the refrigerator.

SAUSAGE AND EGG 'MCDONBURI'

SŌSĒJI EGGU MAFIN DON ソーセージエッグマフィン丼

SERVES 2

Sometime last year, I had a big night out, and I did myself a solid by preparing a good Japanese breakfast for the following morning ahead of time. But when that morning came, my hangover demanded what my hangover usually demands: a McDonald's breakfast. Say what you will about McDonald's, but the sausage and egg McMuffin is undeniably one of the world's most perfect foods. Especially after something like seven Sidecars and a bottle of wine.

So, I ordered my McMuffin to be delivered, but the smell of freshly-steamed rice in the cooker still beckoned. I soon realised I needed the plain, pure comfort of white rice as well. Feeling a bit chaotic-evil, I took the sausage, egg and cheese from between the muffin and plonked it on top of a bowl of rice, then doused the whole thing in a huge spoonful of my friend MiMi's exceptional Burmese chilli oil. And all was right in the world.

Here is a recipe to recreate this extraordinary breakfast (or dinner) bowl, but to be honest, you could just do what I did – order a Maccy D's and put it on rice. Have the muffin for dessert.

Form the sausages into patties no thicker than about 7 mm (¼ in). Melt the butter in a large frying pan over medium-high heat. When the butter is foamy, fry the sausages for about 3–4 minutes until browned, then flip over and add a slice of American cheese to the top of each patty. At the same time, fry the eggs in the same pan – if you have ring moulds (7–9 cm/3–3½ in in diameter), crack the eggs into them to get that nice, round, McDonald's-y shape. Season the eggs with salt and pepper as they fry. After a few minutes, remove the ring moulds, if using, flip the eggs over and cook for just another minute, so the top sets – one of the benefits of making your own McMuffin filling is that you can keep the yolk runny.

Place each egg on top of each cheesed sausage patty, then remove from the heat. Pile beds of rice into bowls, and place the sausage and egg stacks on top of them. Spoon over the chilli oil, as well as a little soy sauce or tonkatsu sauce, if using, and serve hot. This technically lasts for five days in the refrigerator, but the egg and cheese go rubbery if you reheat them, so it's best to eat this one fresh.

2 sausages, squeezed from their cases
    or 150–200 g (5–7 oz) sausagemeat
a little butter
2 eggs
salt and pepper, as needed
2 (American) cheese slices
2 portions of cooked rice
2–4 teaspoons crispy chilli oil (or more,
    if you like)
soy sauce or tonkatsu sauce, as needed

CHICKEN AND ROOT VEGETABLE STEW

CHIKUZEN-NI 筑前煮

SERVES **4**

6 (10–12 g/½ oz) dried shiitake mushrooms
150 ml (5 fl oz/scant ⅔ cup) just-boiled water
2 carrots
12–15 cm (5–6 in) lotus root or 200 g (7 oz)
   (drained weight) tinned water chestnuts
100 g (3½ oz) burdock, Jerusalem
   artichoke or parsnips, scrubbed clean
water with a splash of vinegar added,
   as needed
4–5 *eddoes* (*satoimo/taro*), or 200 g (7 oz)
   waxy potatoes
250 g (9 oz) *konnyaku*
4 chicken thigh fillets
½ teaspoon oil
¼ teaspoon sesame oil
400 ml (13 fl oz/generous 1½ cups) dashi
6 tablespoons soy sauce
2 tablespoons sake
2 tablespoons mirin
1 tablespoon sugar
handful of sugar snap peas or mangetout
   (snow peas)

I have a great fondness for this dish, because it was one of the first things I learned to cook in Japan, at a community cooking class in the city where I lived. It remains one of my favourites particularly because it is one of those ideal 'make ahead' meals that actually improves with time in the refrigerator; the vegetables soak up the dashi, and the seasonings all mellow and mingle to make every mouthful taste fuller, softer and more laden with umami goodness. This recipe contains some somewhat obscure ingredients that will require a trip to an East Asian supermarket – I encourage you to make that trip but, if you can't, I have provided substitutes.

Place the mushrooms in a small bowl and pour over the just-boiled water. Leave to rehydrate for 15 minutes while you prepare the rest of the dish. Peel the carrots and lotus root. Cut the lotus root lengthways into quarters, so you have four prism-shaped batons of lotus root. Cut the lotus root, burdock and carrot into bite-size wedges using a technique called *rangiri* ('chaos cut'): slice at an angle and, with every cut, rotate the vegetable 90 degrees so you end up with pieces that are shaped sort of like big fangs. Keep the lotus root and burdock in the bowl of vinegared water to prevent them browning until ready to cook. Peel the eddoes, cut them into bite-size wedges and add to the vinegared water. Tear the konnyaku into irregular bite-size chunks and keep in the vinegared water. Squeeze the mushrooms dry and save their liquid. Discard the mushroom stems and cut their caps in half.

   Cut the chicken into 2.5 cm (1 in) chunks. In a large saucepan, heat the oils over a medium heat and tip in the chicken, then stir-fry for about 6 minutes until the chicken is lightly browned. Thoroughly drain the vegetables and konnyaku, then add to the saucepan along with the carrots, eddoes and mushrooms. Stir-fry for another few minutes, then add the dashi and all of the seasonings. Bring to a high simmer, skimming off any scum that comes to the surface with a small fine-mesh sieve or a spoon. Once all the scum has been removed, cover with a lid that fits inside the pan, directly on the surface of the ingredients, or with a circle of parchment paper. Keep at a high simmer and cook for about 10 minutes until the eddoes are totally tender – the rest of the veg should still have a bit of bite to them. Finally, stir in the pea pods and cook for another minute or two, then remove from the heat and serve hot. This is a fairly satisfying one-pot meal, but you may wish to have it with rice and pickles. This keeps for five days in the refrigerator.

STEAK BOWL WITH WARISHITA BUTTER SAUCE

TOKUSEI GYŪDON 特製牛丼

SERVES 2

a few drops of sesame oil
4 tablespoons soy sauce
2 egg yolks
3 tablespoons sake
3 tablespoons water
2 tablespoons mirin
1 tablespoon brown sugar
½ teaspoon dashi powder
1 very large steak, or two smaller ones
    – about 400 g (14 oz) in total, any cut
    you like
salt and pepper, as needed
oil, as needed
10 g (½ oz) butter; more if you're using
    quite lean steak, or if you just really
    like butter
2 portions of cooked rice
handful of chives, finely chopped (optional)
wasabi, to taste (optional)
pickled ginger, to garnish

Warishita is the name of a sauce made by seasoning dashi with generous quantities of soy sauce, sake, mirin and sugar. It is sort of like the lovechild of teriyaki sauce and tsuyu, most commonly used in the perennially popular beef hotpot, sukiyaki. Here, it is used to deglaze the pan after frying a steak, then mixed with butter and topped with an egg yolk for a truly decadent take on the humble *gyūdon* (beef bowl).

Grease a couple of ramekins or similar small containers with sesame oil, then divide 1 tablespoon soy sauce between them. Carefully place the egg yolks in each cup and leave to cure lightly while you prepare the rest of the meal.

Combine the remaining 3 tablespoons soy sauce with the sake, water, mirin, sugar and dashi powder and stir well to dissolve. Season the steak on all sides with salt and pepper. In a lightly oiled frying pan (skillet) set over a high heat, cook the steak to your liking – if you're going for a very thick steak, this should take about 10 minutes, turning the steak every minute. Remember to err on the side of rare – if you cut into it and it's not done, you can keep cooking it, but if it's overdone, there's no going back.

Remove the steak from the pan and remove the pan from the heat. Leave the pan to cool slightly, then add the sauce and bring to the boil. Add the butter and whisk it into the sauce as it melts. Keep the sauce at a low simmer until ready to serve. Slice the steak very thinly and arrange the slices in a circle on top of each bowl of hot rice. Place an egg yolk in the middle of each bowl, then spoon over the sauce. Garnish with the chopped chives and a dab of wasabi and pickled ginger on the side, if using, and serve piping hot. This lasts up to three days in the refrigerator, but it's really best eaten immediately.

SEARED SALMON AND SALMON ROE DONBURI WITH WASABI PONZU

KAISEN OYAKODON 海鮮親子丼

SERVES **2**

200–250 g (7–9 oz) salmon, scaled
    and pin-boned
salt, as needed
2 tablespoons oil
3 tablespoons ponzu
1 tablespoon mirin
1 teaspoon sesame oil
¼–½ teaspoon wasabi
50 g (2 oz) salmon roe
2 portions of cooked rice
handful of chives, finely sliced
2 pinches of sesame seeds
pickled ginger, as needed

Oyakodon, a classic dish of chicken and eggs on rice, has a somewhat disturbing name if you translate it directly: 'parent and child bowl'. I mean, I know that description is perfectly accurate, but it's also a bit weird. This dish could also have the same name, as it contains both salmon and salmon roe. Call it what you want – I just call it delicious.

Remove the skin from the salmon but keep the skin. Pat both the salmon and skin dry with paper towel, then season both with salt on all sides. Heat the oil in a frying pan (skillet) over a medium heat and lower in the skin. Fry the skin for about 10 minutes, turning frequently, like you would bacon, until it is very crisp. Remove the crispy skin and drain it on paper towel, and turn the heat up to high on the pan. When the pan is smoking hot, add the salmon and cook for just a minute on each side, so it sears lightly but remains raw inside (you can also use a blowtorch for this). Remove the salmon and transfer to the refrigerator to chill completely. Meanwhile, make a dressing by stirring together the ponzu, mirin, sesame oil and wasabi, ensuring no lumps of wasabi remain. When the salmon is well chilled, use a very sharp knife to cut it into 1 cm (½ in) slices or chunks (like you would for sashimi or poke). Scoop the rice into bowls, and place the salmon on top of it. Add the salmon roe in the middle and garnish with the chives, sesame and crispy salmon skin. To serve, pour over the ponzu dressing and mix everything up. Enjoy with pickled ginger. This will last a couple of days in the refrigerator but is best eaten fresh.

SMALL SIDES

BIG SIDES

RICE BOWL
TOPPINGS

ONE-DISH
DINNERS

PORK BELLY BOWL WITH SALTED LEEK RELISH

NEGISHIO BUTADON ネギ塩豚丼

SERVES 4

2 baby leeks, very finely chopped
3 tablespoons sesame oil
1 tablespoon lemon juice
1 tablespoon mirin
1 garlic clove, minced
½ teaspoon salt, plus more, to taste
½ teaspoon chicken stock powder
lots and lots of freshly ground pepper
450–500 g (1 lb–1 lb 2 oz) pork belly,
   rind off
a little oil, for greasing
2 portions of cooked rice

Negishio is a delicious and versatile relish made primarily from *negi* (leeks) and *shio* (salt) as well as copious amounts of sesame oil and a few other seasonings. I believe it is originally derived from the spring onion-based dipping sauces and marinades found in Korean barbecue and it is used similarly in Japanese cooking, often accompanying rich grilled meats such as beef tongue or pork belly. The sharp flavour of raw leeks is the perfect accent to fatty pork, and if you have it on rice, the sauce and the juices from the meat dribble down to coat the grains, making for an incredibly moreish mouthful.

Combine all the ingredients except the pork belly, oil for greasing and cooked rice and stir well. Slice the pork belly very thinly – think bacon rashers. You may want to put the pork in the freezer for 30 minutes prior to slicing, which will firm it up and make it easier to cut. Cut the slices of pork belly in half, so they are roughly bite-size. Lightly oil a baking tray (pan), using some paper towel to spread the oil around in an even layer. Lay the pork belly slices out in a single layer, then place under a very hot grill (broiler) for about 5-6 minutes until browned on one side. Turn the pork belly over and grill for another 4–5 minutes until the other side is browned, too. If there are any juices in the tray, tip them into the negishio sauce and stir well, then taste and adjust the seasoning as necessary with more salt. To serve, lay the pork belly on top of the rice in deep bowls, then spoon over the relish. Serve hot or at room temperature. This lasts five days in the refrigerator.

CRAB AND SPINACH DORIA

KANI TO HŌRENSŌ NO EIFŪ DORIA 蟹とほうれん草の英風ドリア

SERVES 2 OR UP TO 4 WITH OTHER DISHES

People who assume all Japanese food is light and fresh are often taken aback by doria, an indulgent rice gratin that first gained popularity in Yokohama in the 1930s. Nowadays, doria are firmly part of the *yōshoku* canon and are made with a very wide variety of toppings. This recipe might more correctly be called a gratin rather than a doria, because doria contain a sauce – béchamel, tomato, Bolognese, curry, etc. In this case, a generous amount of cream is mixed with the crab, spinach and cheese topping, so it sort of self-sauces as it melts. Whatever you call it, it's *really* good – an incredibly indulgent and satisfying meal.

Preheat a fan oven to 180°C (350°F/gas 4). Mix together all of the ingredients except the butter, rice, egg and parsley. Ensure everything is well combined and in particular be mindful that there are no un-mixed lumps of miso. Lightly grease a gratin dish with the butter, then press the cooked rice into the base of the dish in a compact, solid layer. Scoop an egg-sized divot out of the middle of the rice and crack the egg into it. Spoon the crabby cheese mix over the entire surface of the rice – take care when covering the egg, so that you don't break the yolk. This can now be covered and refrigerated until ready to cook and serve, for up to three days. If you've just assembled this using hot or warm rice, bake the gratin in the oven for 18 minutes; if you've used cold rice, or prepped the whole thing ahead and taken it out of the refrigerator, bake for 22 minutes until the cheese has melted and lightly browned, but the egg is still runny. Garnish with the chopped parsley just before serving while still piping hot.

150 g (5 oz) crab meat (half-half white and brown meat is ideal)
120 g (4 oz) frozen spinach, defrosted and squeezed dry (or about 180 g (6⅓ oz) fresh spinach, blanched, squeezed dry and chopped)
70 g (2½ oz) grated (shredded) mozzarella
30 g (1 oz) grated (shredded) Emmental
1 tablespoon grated (shredded) Parmesan
1 spring onion (scallion), finely chopped
1 garlic clove, grated
4 tablespoons double (heavy) cream
2 tablespoons miso
1 tablespoon sake
1 teaspoon Dijon mustard
2 teaspoons Worcestershire sauce
dash of hot sauce
several shakes of Old Bay (optional)
quite a lot of pepper
a little butter, for greasing
2 portions of cooked rice
1 egg
flat-leaf parsley leaves, finely chopped, to garnish

SPAGHETTI NAPOLITAN

SUPAGETTĪ NAPORITAN スパゲッティーナポリタン

SERVES 2 GENEROUSLY, OR 3–4 CHILDREN

1 knob (about 2 tablespoons) butter
1 onion, halved and finely sliced
1 (bell) pepper, finely sliced
100–150 g (3½–5 oz) mushrooms, sliced
2 hot dogs, cut into 1 cm (½ in) thick
    pieces at an angle (if you can get
    Japanese wieners, they are fantastic,
    but they are small, so use 4 instead of 2)
salt, as needed
250 g (9 oz) spaghetti
1 garlic clove, finely chopped
4 tablespoons ketchup
2 tablespoons soy sauce
1 tablespoon Worcestershire sauce
pepper, to taste
Tabasco sauce, to taste (optional)
Parmesan, to taste

I've been sitting on this recipe for a while, as it was originally included in the pitch for my previous book on *izakaya* food. I wanted that book to include a chapter on *kissaten*, old-school coffee shops that I often think of as the daytime counterpart to izakaya. They have similarly laid-back vibes, with a focus on drinks (in this case, caffeine instead of alcohol) and varying levels of second-hand smoke. They're not quite as sociable as izakaya, and the food isn't meant for sharing, but it's a similar mix of old and new, East and West, and nostalgic and novel. Curry rice, pizza toast and egg sandwiches are the purview of kissaten, as are mid-century *wafū* pasta dishes such as the classic spaghetti 'Napolitan'. Of course, this has basically nothing to do with Napoli, or really anywhere in Italy, and everything to do with America, for it was the American post-war occupation that brought so many of this dish's key ingredients: the hot dogs, the ketchup and the wheat flour to make the pasta itself. Thanks to its crowd-pleasing nature, this also pops up in restaurants as a component of the kids' set meal known as an *okosama* lunch.

Melt the butter in a deep frying pan (skillet) set over a medium heat. Add the onion, pepper, mushrooms and hot dogs, and sauté for about 8–10 minutes until the onions are lightly browned. Meanwhile, bring a large saucepan full of water to the boil and add a few big pinches of salt. Add the pasta and cook according to the package instructions. Meanwhile, add the garlic to the frying pan and sauté until softened, then add the ketchup, soy sauce, Worcestershire sauce and pepper. Let the liquid come to the boil, then add a ladle full of the pasta water and let it come to the boil again. When the pasta is al dente, drain it and tip it into the frying pan. Add a dash or two of Tabasco, if using, and use tongs to mix the pasta through the sauce, keeping the heat on so it reduces as you mix. Garnish with finely grated Parmesan. You can serve this at any temperature. It lasts for five days in the refrigerator, but does not reheat well – enjoy the leftovers cold.

ONE-PAN WAFŪ MUSHROOM PASTA

NABE HITOTSU DE TSUKURERU KINOKO SHŌYU BATĀ WAFŪ PASUTA

鍋一つで作れるきのこ醤油バター和風パスタ

SERVES 4

40 g (1½ oz) butter
1 tablespoon olive oil
400 g (14 oz) Japanese mushrooms –
    such as shiitake, shimeji, eryngi, enoki
    or oyster, destemmed, cleaned and cut
    into bite-size pieces
4 garlic cloves, finely chopped
200 g (7 oz) fresh spinach (not baby
    spinach, if possible), washed and
    roughly chopped
4 tablespoons soy sauce
400 g (14 oz) spaghetti
1 tablespoon mirin
½ teaspoon dashi powder
pepper, to taste
flat-leaf parsley leaves, finely chopped,
    to garnish
1 sheet of nori, cut into 4 strips and then
    into fine shreds with kitchen scissors

What makes something *wafū*? The word means 'Japanese style', so to answer this question, we have to consider the defining characteristics of Japanese culinary aesthetics. Or do we? Japanese conbini sell 'wafū' tuna mayo onigiri and sandwiches, which is just tuna mayo with added soy sauce and dashi. Likewise, wafū pasta is just pasta made with Japanese flavours, such as miso, umeboshi or *mentaiko*. It's funny, because it would be absurd if I or any other non-Japanese person declared that a dish was 'Japanese style' just because I added a few Japanese ingredients. But when the term is used by the Japanese, it becomes indicative of what could be considered to be important or distinctive about their own food. And maybe that's not anything abstract or philosophical – maybe it's just the flavours that are the most familiar. And that can still be a very powerful thing.

So this pasta isn't very different from something you might actually find in Italy, but the inclusion of soy sauce, nori and dashi does, in my mind, place it firmly in Japanese territory.

Melt half of the butter in a saucepan large enough to cook the pasta in as well. Add the olive oil, mushrooms and garlic and cook over a medium-high heat for about 6 minutes until browned and slightly softened. Add the spinach and half the soy sauce and cook for another 2–3 minutes until the spinach is fully wilted. Scrape everything out of the pan and into a bowl or container. Fill the pan with water and bring to the boil, then add the spaghetti and cook until done, according to the package instructions (about 9–11 minutes). Drain well, but save about 100 ml (3½ fl oz/scant ½ cup) of the pasta water. Mix the remaining soy sauce into the pasta water along with the mirin and dashi powder. Return the pasta to the pan along with the pasta water mixture, the mushrooms and spinach. Over a medium heat, stir everything together to combine, adding lots of pepper as you go. When the sauce has thickened, remove from the heat and add the remaining butter, stirring to melt it through the sauce. Garnish with the parsley, the nori shreds and more pepper, if you like, and serve hot. This lasts for three days in the refrigerator, but is better eaten fresh.

'SOUP'S NOT A MEAL! YOU'RE SUPPOSED TO BUY ME A MEAL!'

Kenny Bania

CHEESY CURRY HOTPOT UDON

CHĪZU KARĒ NABEYAKI UDON チーズカレー鍋焼きうどん

SERVES **2**

800 ml (28 fl oz/3½ cups) just-boiled water
4 (6–8 g/¼ oz) dried shiitake mushrooms
1 tablespoon Worcestershire sauce
1 teaspoon chicken stock powder
½ teaspoon dashi powder
80 g (3 oz) Japanese curry roux,
    finely chopped
2 big handfuls (about 80 g/3 oz) of kale,
    destemmed and roughly torn or chopped
2 baby leeks or 4 spring onions (scallions),
    cut into 1 cm (½ in)-thick slices at an angle
2 portions of udon (fresh or frozen, not dried)
1 egg (or 2, if you're making two
    individual portions)
50 g (2 oz) mozzarella or mild
    Cheddar, grated
20 g (¾ oz) fried tofu (abura-age or tofu
    puffs), cut into pieces about an inch
    wide (optional)
100–150 g (3½–5 oz) firm tofu, cut into
    1 cm (½ in)-thick slices

Nabeyaki udon is udon cooked and served in a small hotpot (a *nabe*), with a wide variety of toppings and regional variations. Because the noodles, broth and toppings are all cooked together in the same vessel, it's one of the easiest Japanese noodle dishes to prepare, as well as one of the most warming and satisfying. Even more so if you combine it with cheesy curry, because cheesy curry makes everything better.

Combine the water and mushrooms in a medium-sized (about 22 cm/8⅔ in diameter, 1.5 litre/52 fl oz/6¼ cup capacity) hotpot or casserole and leave to soak while you prepare the rest of the ingredients. When the mushrooms have rehydrated fully, squeeze them dry and discard their stems. Bring the water to a high simmer and add the Worcestershire sauce, chicken stock powder, dashi powder and curry roux. Use a whisk to dissolve the roux, then add the mushrooms, kale and leeks. Boil for about 4 minutes until the veg are tender, then add the udon. Let the liquid come back to the boil, then crack the egg into the centre of the soup and top with the cheese. Place a lid on the pan and cook for another 3–4 minutes so the egg sets and the cheese melts. Top with the tofu and serve immediately – ideally, this should still be bubbling when you tuck in.

NOTE   This recipe gives instructions to cook two servings together in one pot, but it's much better if you can make each portion in its own smaller pot (and this way everybody gets their own egg!). So, if you happen to have two smaller nabe or casserole (about 20 cm/8 in in diameter, 700 ml/24 fl oz/scant 3 cups capacity each), then divide the ingredients between them and cook them separately.

ONE-PAN PEANUT BUTTER TANTANMEN

HAYAKUTE KANTAN NI DEKIRU PĪNATSU BATĀ TANTANMEN

速くて簡単に出来るピーナツバター担々麺

SERVES 2

2 portions of ramen or egg noodles
  (or any Chinese-style wheat noodle)
1 large or 2 small pak choi (bok choi),
  washed and quartered
50 g (2 oz) bean sprouts
1 tablespoon oil
150 g (5 oz) minced (ground) pork
1 cm (½ in) fresh ginger root, peeled
  and finely chopped
1½ tablespoons red miso
1½ tablespoons Shaoxing wine
¼ teaspoon sanshō or finely ground
  Sichuan pepper
¼ teaspoon black pepper
550 ml (19⅓ fl oz/scant 2⅓ cups)
  chicken stock
70 g (2½ oz) peanut butter
2 teaspoons Korean chilli (hot pepper) flakes
1 tablespoon sesame oil
½ teaspoon minced garlic
2 tablespoons soy sauce, plus more, to taste
1 tablespoon mirin
½ teaspoon vinegar
2 teaspoons sesame seeds
2 spring onions (scallions), finely sliced
lots of chilli oil, to taste

Tantanmen, the Japanese iteration of Sichuanese dan dan noodles, is one of the best 'quick' ramen dishes to make at home, because so much of its flavour and body comes from added seasonings rather than lengthy simmers and infusions. With this recipe, I wanted to keep it as quick and simple as possible, so everything is done in one pan – even the washing up is easy. Traditional tantanmen is made from roasted sesame paste, but peanut butter is not without precedent and a more than adequate substitute, something I discovered when I had a tantanmen craving but no sesame paste was in the house.

In a large saucepan, cook the ramen according to the package instructions, but stop just short of al dente – they should be a little undercooked. In the final minute of cooking, add the pak choi and bean sprouts. Drain and rinse the noodles and vegetables well under cold water to remove excess starch and halt the cooking. Separate the pak choi from the noodles and bean sprouts, then set everything aside while you make the rest of the dish.

Rinse and wipe out the saucepan you used to cook the noodles (no need to wash it properly). Set the pan over a medium-high heat and add the oil. Add the pork mince and ginger and stir-fry for about 6 minutes until cooked through and beginning to brown. Stir in the miso, Shaoxing wine and peppers and continue to cook until the liquid is totally reduced. Remove from the heat and scrape the mince into a container. Pour the chicken stock into the pan along with the peanut butter, Korean chilli, sesame oil, garlic, soy sauce, mirin and vinegar. Bring to the boil and use a whisk or stick blender to blend the peanut butter into the broth (which method you use will depend on the consistency of your peanut butter). Taste and adjust the seasoning with soy sauce as needed.

To serve, return the noodles and bean sprouts to the broth for a minute or so to re-warm them, then remove from the heat. Divide the noodles and broth into two ramen bowls and top with the pork mince, pak choi, sesame seeds, spring onions and chilli oil – lots and lots of chilli oil. Slurp while it's piping hot! This can however last for up to three days in the refrigerator if you keep the broth separate from the noodles and toppings.

ONE-PAN CHANPON

HITOTSUNABE DE TSUKURU CHANPON 一つ鍋で作るちゃんぽん

SERVES 2

1 tablespoon lard or vegetable oil
80 g (3 oz) pork (any cut) or chicken thigh,
    finely sliced
1 small onion, finely sliced
½ sweetheart (hispi) cabbage,
    roughly chopped
3 spring onions (scallions), cut into
    1-in chunks
80 g (3 oz) bean sprouts
½ carrot, halved and cut into thin planks
1 tablespoon sesame oil
2 pinches of white pepper
100 g (3 ½ oz) raw prawns (shrimp),
    shelled and deveined
80 g (3 oz) squid, cut into 1 cm rings or strips
60 g (2 oz) scallops
40 g (1½ oz) *kamaboko* or similar fish cake
    (optional), cut into 5 mm (¼ in) slices
1 litre (34 fl oz/4 cups) chicken stock
100 ml (3½ fl oz/scant ½ cup) milk
1 tablespoon soy sauce
1 tablespoon sake
½ teaspoon MSG
¼ teaspoon salt, or more, to taste
2 portions (about 200 g/7 oz) of dried
    ramen or egg noodles
red pickled ginger, to garnish (optional)

Chanpon is a speciality of Nagasaki which is thought to be a sort of proto-ramen, originally invented circa 1890 by the Fujianese chef Chen Pingjun at his restaurant Shikairō, which is still operating in Nagasaki today. In his indispensable history of ramen, *Slurp!*, Professor Barak Kushner describes the original chanpon as 'essentially a seasoned dish of leftovers into which he threw everything not used that day, usually with some kind of meat, and stirring in some noodles and soup mix'. That pretty well covers it; 'chanpon' translates as 'jumble' or 'mixture', and indeed it is an unfussy noodle soup piled high with a mishmash of colourful vegetables and seafood. It is usually prepared by cooking the noodles and toppings separately, then combining everything with the broth – a three-pan affair. But this can all be done in the same pan and the results are similar. In fact, the starch from the noodles will give the broth more body, which is ideal, as chanpon restaurants use a creamy pork-and-chicken stock that clings to the noodles and toppings beautifully.

In a very large saucepan, heat the lard or oil over a high heat. Stir-fry the pork until it is cooked through, then add all of the vegetables, sesame oil and a big pinch of salt. Continue to stir-fry for another 4–5 minutes until they have wilted but remain crunchy. Add the white pepper and shellfish and stir-fry for another 4–5 minutes until cooked through. Tip everything out into a bowl.

Add the chicken stock, milk and seasonings to the pan and bring to the boil. Add the noodles and cook until they're about 2 minutes shy of al dente, using the package instructions as a guide. At this point, return the vegetables and shellfish to the pan and a big pinch of salt. Continue to boil for a couple of minutes until they are warmed through and the noodles are cooked. Taste the broth and adjust the seasoning with more salt and pepper, if you like. Divide everything into deep ramen bowls and garnish with pickled ginger, if using. Serve hot and eat immediately.

SOBA, MANGETOUT AND TARRAGON SALAD WITH CARROT-MISO DRESSING

SOBA, SAYA-ENDŌ TO TARAGON SARADA, NINJIN DORESSHINGU AE

そば、サヤエンドウとタラゴンのサラダ、人参ドレッシング和え

SERVES 2

Tarragon is not traditionally used in Japanese cooking, but its vibrant, fennel-y flavour works well in many Japanese preparations. If you can get young tarragon with tender stems, it makes exceptional tempura, for example. I think it also works well with soba, providing an uplifting aroma that works well with the nuttiness of buckwheat. I made a salad similar to this one for my *MasterChef* audition and that turned out pretty well for me, so I guess this salad is a certified winner!

To make the dressing, combine all the ingredients in a blender and purée until as smooth as possible. Fill a large saucepan with water and bring to the boil. Cook the soba according to the package instructions – usually this involves a quick boil followed by simmering at a lower temperature, generally anywhere from 3–8 minutes in total. When there's 1 minute left on the soba, add the mangetout to the pan and cook for a final minute. Drain in a sieve and rinse thoroughly under cold water to remove excess starch, then drain very well and toss with the sesame oil. To serve, spoon some dressing on top of the noodles and garnish with the tarragon leaves and sesame. If you keep the dressing separate, this will last for three days in the refrigerator.

For the Dressing

½ medium carrot, peeled and
　roughly chopped
3 mm (⅛ in) slice of fresh ginger root, peeled
2 tablespoons white miso
2 tablespoons water
2 tablespoons mirin
2 tablespoons vinegar
2 tablespoons olive oil

For the Salad

2 portions (200 g/7 oz) of dried
　soba noodles
100 g (3½ oz) mangetout (snow peas)
1 teaspoon sesame oil
a few sprigs of tarragon, leaves picked
a few pinches of sesame seeds

BLT HIYASHI RAMEN SALAD WITH TERIYAKI BUTTER MAYO DRESSING

BLT HIYASHI CHŪKA BLT冷やし中華

SERVES **2**

2 medium tomatoes (about 100 g/3½ oz
    each), cored, halved and sliced about
    7 mm (¼ in) thick
MSG and sea salt, as needed
6 rashers of smoked streaky bacon
1 garlic clove, smashed
3 pound-coin (just under an inch)-sized
    slices of fresh ginger root
3 tablespoons soy sauce
1 tablespoon sake
1 tablespoon mirin
1 tablespoon honey
¼ teaspoon cornflour (cornstarch)
20 g (¾ oz) butter
1 tablespoon lemon juice
6 tablespoons mayonnaise
2 portions of ramen noodles
2 huge handfuls (a little less than half
    a head) of iceberg lettuce, shredded
handful of chives, finely sliced
a few big pinches of sesame seeds

I had a BLT from the café in our local park the other day and, my GOD, was it good. I'd had so many bad BLTs over the years that I'd forgotten how truly fantastic they can be. At their best, they contain a perfect balance of contrasting flavours and textures – in many ways, they are unimprovable. However, I have long held the belief that most things, if not all things, would be better if they were ramen. To put that theory to the test, here is a BLT, in ramen salad format.

Sprinkle the tomato slices with a few pinches of MSG and sea salt. Fry the bacon in a frying pan (skillet) over a medium-low heat until it is very crisp and brown. Drain on paper towel and tip the bacon grease into a small bowl. Add the garlic, ginger, soy sauce, sake, mirin and honey to a small saucepan and bring to a high simmer, and continue to simmer for 4–5 minutes. Stir together the cornflour with a little water to make a thin slurry, then stir this into the saucepan as well. Bring back to a simmer and cook until the sauce thickens, then remove from the heat and add the butter and bacon grease, whisking to emulsify into the sauce. Add the lemon juice, and leave to cool to room temperature while you prepare the rest of the dish. When the sauce has cooled, remove the ginger and garlic and whisk the sauce into the mayonnaise, then keep in the refrigerator until ready to serve.

Cook the noodles according to the package instructions, but give them an extra 30 seconds or so, as they will firm up when you chill them. Rinse the noodles well under cold running water, tossing them with your hands as you go to remove excess starch.

To serve, place the noodles into wide, shallow bowls, and top with the lettuce, tomatoes, chives and sesame. Use your hands to crumble the bacon on top. Drizzle over the teriyaki mayo. Give everything a good mix before devouring. This will last for up to three days in the refrigerator if you keep everything separate until ready to eat.

CHEESY YAKISOBA OMELETTE

CHĪZU OMUSOBA チーズオムそば

SERVES 1 (SEE RECIPE INTRODUCTION)

2 tablespoons oil
60 g (2 oz) pork (any cut), finely sliced
½ onion, finely sliced
½ carrot, peeled and finely sliced into
    little planks
¼ sweetheart (hispi) cabbage, cut into
    1 cm (½ in)-thick strips
1 portion of egg noodles, fresh or par-boiled
1 tablespoon water
1 tablespoon soy sauce
1 tablespoon sake
1 tablespoon mirin
½ tablespoon Worcestershire sauce
pinch of pepper
2 eggs
1 tablespoon milk
¼ teaspoon dashi powder
pinch of salt
40 g (1½ oz) mild melting cheese
    (such as mozzarella or Edam), grated
Japanese brown sauce (ideally
    okonomiyaki or takoyaki sauce),
    or ketchup, as needed (about 30 g/1 oz)
mayonnaise, as needed (about 15 g/½ oz)
lots of chives, finely sliced

Omusoba is a kind of mash-up of *omurice* and yakisoba, i.e., stir-fried noodles bundled up in a blanket of egg. Variations abound, but my favourite (of course) is the kind with cheese inside, which pushes all of my nostalgia buttons. See, yakisoba was one of the first Japanese dishes I learned to cook as a teenager, and cheesy omelettes remind me of weekend trips to local diners with my dad. So, for me,this is some seriously comforting comfort food. Because everything here has to fit inside one omelette, this does not scale up very well. However, if you do want to make more than one serving, you can make a big batch of the noodles, and then just make multiple omelettes one at a time, dividing the noodles between them as you go.

Heat 1 tablespoon oil in a frying pan (skillet) over a high heat, then add the pork, onion and carrot and stir-fry for about 3 minutes until lightly browned. Add the cabbage and continue to stir-fry for about 5 minutes until wilted. Add the noodles along with all of the liquid seasonings and the pepper and stir-fry for a couple of minutes until everything is well mixed and the liquid has become completely absorbed into the noodles. Line a plate with cling film (plastic wrap), then tip the yakisoba into the centre of it, and wrap it up like a sort of noodle log. Keep under a tea towel (dishcloth) to keep warm while you prepare the rest of the dish.

    Beat the eggs very well with the milk, dashi powder and salt. Heat the 1 teaspoon oil in a large, separate frying pan over medium heat, then pour in the egg. Cook on one side until set on the bottom, then lay the cheese across the middle of the omelette. Carefully unwrap the yakisoba onto the noodles, so that it remains in a log-like form, and draw up the sides of the omelette to enclose the noodles in a duvet of egg. Tip the omusoba onto a plate, cheesy side up, and garnish with the brown sauce, mayonnaise and chives. You can serve this at any temperature, although hot is best. It lasts for three days in the refrigerator.

HOT SOBA WITH DUCK AND BABY LEEKS
KAMO NANBAN SOBA 鴨南蛮そば

SERVES 2

1 teaspoon oil
1 (about 200 g/7 oz) duck breast
salt, as needed
4 baby leeks or ½ regular leek, cut into
    1 cm (½ in)-thick slices at an angle
600 ml (20 fl oz/2½ cups) dashi
4 tablespoons soy sauce
3 tablespoons mirin
2 portions (200 g/7 oz) of dried soba noodles
flat-leaf parsley leaves, to garnish
about ½ teaspoon finely grated citrus zest
    – any kind will do, but bergamot is very
    lovely, if you can get it
shichimi pepper and/or wasabi,
    to taste (optional)

NOTE   I learned of an alternative
method for cooking the duck from
videos I've watched of two of the
oldest Nanban soba specialists in
Japan: Soba Dokoro Okina in Aomori
and Kamo Nanban Honke in Kanagawa.
Instead of frying a whole duck breast
and then slicing it, instead these shops
slice the duck first, very thinly, and
fry it like bacon before poaching it
in the dashi along with the onions.
If I'm honest, I do not think the results
of this method are as good as pan-
roasting, but it is much quicker, and
lends a nice duckiness to the broth.

The great cookery instructor and author Reiko Hashimoto
posted about *nanban soba* on Instagram, tagging me to see
if I knew the origins of its name of this classic dish. Nanban
is the name of my first book and the restaurant I ran for more
than six years, which I chose because of how well it describes
who I am and what I cook. It means 'southern barbarian',
an epithet applied to Europeans when they first arrived in
Japan centuries ago, and persists as a name for certain
dishes that were introduced or influenced by these early
missionaries and traders, often specialities of Kyushu,
where I lived in Japan.

But I did not know the origins of nanban soba until Reiko
prompted me to investigate. There are two compelling
theories. One has to do with the inclusion of onions or
leeks; while nanban soba was only invented in the 19th
century, the earlier *nanban-ni* referred to meat boiled with
onions and peppers, which were considered hallmarks of
nanban cookery and also feature in the classic *nanban-zuke*
(escabeche). Another theory suggests that this dish gained
the nanban name because it features pan-frying in oil, seen
as novel and European at the time.

It's interesting, because now nanban soba is about
200 years old, and it presents as a very traditional, very
'Japanese' dish, yet its name still carries the baggage of
foreign influence in Japan.

Pour the oil into a frying pan (skillet) and place over a low
heat. Season the duck breast with salt and fry, skin side
down, for about 15 minutes until the fat is rendered and
the skin is golden brown. Turn the duck over and cook
for 6–7 minutes. This should yield a medium-well breast.
Remove the duck and rest on a cutting board, tip out any
excess fat and add the leeks. Turn the heat up to high and
then stir-fry with a pinch of salt for another few minutes
until browned, then remove from the heat. Heat the dashi,
soy sauce and mirin to a simmer in a saucepan, then taste
and adjust the seasoning with additional salt as needed.
Tip the fried leeks into the broth and leave to simmer as
you cook the noodles.

Fill another large saucepan with water and bring to the
boil. Cook the soba according to the package instructions.
While the noodles are cooking, slice the duck. When the
soba is al dente, drain it well, rinse it under warm tap water
to remove excess starch, then divide it into noodle bowls.
Pour over the broth along with the leeks, garnish with the
sliced duck, parsley, citrus zest and shichimi or wasabi,
if using, and serve while hot. This lasts for about three days
in the refrigerator if you keep the cooked noodles, broth
and toppings all in separate containers.

4

BREAD & PASTRIES

素材パン・サンドイッチ・菓子パン

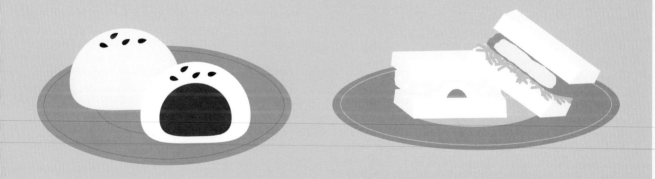

BREAD & PASTRIES

素材パン・サンドイッチ・菓子パン

Towards the back of the conbini is a shelf full of baked goods. Some of it is sweet, some savoury, and it is almost invariably based on some form of squishy white bread. Japanese sandwiches can be found in the chiller cabinets, and they are pleasingly bland. While these items may not be considered 'traditional' Japanese food, they are as much a part of Japan's culinary landscape as anything else, and they make for some excellent lunches.

JAPANESE-STYLE SANDWICH BREAD
SANDOICCHI YŌ NO SHOKUPAN サンドイッチ用の食パン

MAKES **1 LOAF,** TO YIELD **15-18** SLICES

Recently, many home bakers in the Anglosphere have started to make something they call 'Hokkaido milk bread', one of many Japanese food names that have become misapplied outside Japan. In the UK, Hokkaido milk bread refers to a specific white bread made with various dairy products and highly sweetened with honey, sugar or both. However, 'Hokkaido milk bread' in Japan refers to any bread made with milk from Hokkaido, which is famous for dairy products – and it certainly isn't what's used for most Japanese sandwiches. That would be *shokupan*, which is the Japanese word for white bread – literally 'food bread,' a distinction begun in the late 19th century to differentiate bread from pencil erasers, known at the time as 'erasing bread' (*keshipan*).

Shokupan can be made in many ways, with many ingredients, but at its most basic, it can be distinguished from ordinary Western white bread by four key ingredients: sugar, margarine, vitamin C and a pre-cooked starch paste or 'water roux' called *yudane*. Yudane in particular makes the bread softer but also springier. This makes it perfect for sandwiches, especially pre-made ones, which should be soft enough so you can bite through them easily, but also resilient enough to survive any moisture that may leach out of the filling, as well as any damage that may be suffered during transit.

To be honest, if you're in the mood for Japanese convenience store-style sandwiches, you can just use any supermarket white bread, but I do encourage you to try this recipe – it's just so perfect for sando.

You will need a stand mixer with a dough hook and a 12–13 cm (4–5 in)-wide square sandwich loaf tin, ideally with a lid, for this recipe. Also, it is worth noting that this is a two-day process – so if you make the yudane on a Saturday, it won't be fully ready for sando until Monday (see method for details).

For the Yudane (Water Roux)

150 g (5 oz) very strong bread flour
230 g (8 oz) just-boiled water

For the Dough

200 g (7 oz) warm water (around 35–40°C/95–104°F, like bath water)
14 g (½ oz) dried yeast
200 g (7 oz) milk
620 g (1 lb 6 oz) very strong bread flour, plus more for dusting
12 g (½ oz) salt
½ teaspoon vitamin C
40 g (1½ oz) golden caster (superfine) sugar
80 g (3 oz) margarine, diced, plus more for greasing
2 tablespoons double (heavy) cream (optional)

CONT.

To make the yudane, place the flour in a heatproof bowl set over a saucepan of simmering water; this is so the just-boiled water doesn't cool off when you mix it in. As soon as the water boils, pour it into the flour, and quickly stir it together with a wooden spoon. You'll need to grip the side of the bowl with a tea towel (dishcloth) or oven glove, because the bowl will be hot and the mixture will be very tough to stir. When it comes together it should be super thick and sticky, with a consistency somewhere between wallpaper paste and Play-Doh. Remove from the heat and leave to cool to room temperature, then scrape the roux into a container, and cover with a lid or cling film (plastic wrap). Refrigerate overnight.

The next day, take the yudane out of the refrigerator at least an hour before you make the rest of the dough. In a bowl or jug, stir together the warm water and yeast until the yeast dissolves, then add the milk. In the bowl of a stand mixer fitted with the dough hook, combine the flour, salt, vitamin C and sugar. Switch the mixer on to low speed. Pour the liquid into the dry ingredients as it mixes, then tear the yudane into little chunks and drop them into the mixer, one by one. After a few minutes, the dough will come together into a solid if shaggy mass. At this point, add the margarine, piece by piece, and switch the speed up to medium-low (speed 2 on my KitchenAid, for reference), and knead for 20 minutes. Don't wander far from the machine during this time; the dough is very, very tough, and as it bashes around inside the mixing bowl, the machine may become dangerously unstable, gyrating this way and that across the countertop, and when it does this it could knock stuff over or fall off the counter completely. It could also overheat.

Give your mixer a rest if it looks like it might conk out. The main point is to check that your dough passes the 'windowpane test' consistently. What that means is that you should be able to grab a blob of dough and easily stretch it out to a thinness that allows you to see through it. If the dough tears, or stretches into strings rather than sheets, keep kneading. Personally, I think this should be called the 'bubblegum test', because that's the consistency you're looking for – a nice, evenly elastic, translucent dough.

Once your dough has passed this test, tip it out into a bowl greased with margarine, cover loosely with cling film (plastic wrap), and leave in the warmest spot you can find for about an hour until doubled in size.

Lightly grease the sides of a Pullman loaf tin or similar square bread tin with margarine. Turn the dough out onto a very lightly floured surface and divide into three equal pieces – they really should be equal, so I recommend using a scale. The dough should weigh around 1440 g (3 lb 3 oz), so each third should be 480 g (1 lb 1 oz). Roll each piece out into a rectangle roughly as wide as the base of your bread tin, and fold the long edges into the centre to form a narrower rectangle. Roll each rectangle of dough up from the short edge like a long carpet, and place them side-by-side in the base of the tin, with the coiled edges of each roll facing out towards the long sides of the tin. Leave to prove in a warm place until the dough has risen nearly to the top of the tin, shy by about 1 cm (½ in) – keep an eye on this, because the vitamin C will make the yeast very active. Grease the inside of the lid of the tin, if using, and slide it on. If you are not using a lid, brush the top of the dough with double cream.

Preheat a fan oven to 170°C (325°F/gas 3) and bake for 1 hour 10 minutes. When the bread is done, bang the tin on the counter, hard, which apparently 'sets' the gluten structure and helps keep it from collapsing. This sounds like hocus pocus to me, but when I did it, my bread did not collapse, so I wouldn't chance not doing it. Remove the bread from the tin as soon as it is done, and transfer to a wire rack to cool. Do not slice until it is completely cool. At this point, the bread will have a very, very delicate crumb but a robust, crunchy crust. This is delicious, and you should eat a slice now, with softened butter. But it's not good for sandwiches, which requires a firmer crumb and softer crust. So, wrap the bread up in cling film and leave it until the next day. At this point, your shokupan is ready for slicing and sandwiching, and, because of the yudane and vitamin C, it will stay good for several days, if you keep it wrapped up. Once it goes stale, it still makes exquisite toast. The bread can also be pre-sliced and frozen.

BASIC JAPANESE BREAD ROLL DOUGH

KIHON NO RŌRU PAN KIJI 基本のロールパン生地

MAKES ABOUT 620 G (1 LB 6 OZ) – ENOUGH FOR 12 SMALL SWEET BUNS OR 8 LARGER SAVOURY BUNS

Besides shokupan, perhaps the most versatile type of Japanese bread dough is a simple, lightly sweetened white dough which is used for the sweet and savoury rolls that are staples of bakeries, supermarkets and convenience stores. These include sweet red bean buns, hot dog rolls and baked curry bread (recipes follow), as well as custard buns, chocolate cornets, buns filled with whipped cream and jam, and a variety of *sōzai pan*, or savoury side dish buns, that feature Japanese comfort foods like tuna mayo, croquettes or yakisoba in a convenient hand-held bread-based format. The bread is also very nice on its own, soft, pillowy and mildly sweet, so you can just have it with soup or a salad for a light meal. You will need a stand mixer with a dough hook for this recipe.

Mix the yeast and water in a measuring jug until dissolved. Combine the flour, sugar and salt in a stand mixer fitted with a dough hook. Add the milk and egg to the yeasted water, then pour this into the stand mixer while mixing on low speed, then add the honey. When the dough comes together, add the margarine in small pieces and turn the speed up to medium. Knead for about 10 minutes, or until the dough passes the 'window pane' gluten test (see shokupan method, opposite). Place the dough in a lightly buttered bowl, cover loosely with cling film (plastic wrap) or a tea towel (dishcloth), and leave to prove somewhere warm for about an hour, or until doubled in size. Proceed to shape and bake according to the recipes that follow or, to make plain rolls, simply divide the dough into 12 equal pieces (50 g/2 oz each). Place on paper-lined trays, and leave to rise again for 45 minutes– 1 hour before baking in a fan oven at 200°C (400°F/gas 6) for 10 minutes.

7 g (¼ oz) yeast
160 ml (5½ fl oz/⅔ cup) lukewarm water
360 g (12⅔ oz) very strong bread flour
15 g (½ oz) golden caster (superfine) sugar
5 g (¼ oz) salt
1 tablespoon milk
1 egg
1 tablespoon honey
20 g (¾ oz) margarine or butter, plus more for greasing

SWEET RED BEAN BUNS

ANPAN アンパン

MAKES 12 BUNS

2 tins (560–580g/1 lb 4 oz total drained
    weight) of adzuki beans
80–90 g (3 lb ¼ oz) light brown sugar
2 tablespoons honey
1 batch of Basic Japanese Bread Roll
    Dough, page 185
plain (all-purpose) flour, for dusting
1 egg, beaten well with a splash of milk
poppy seeds, to garnish

Perhaps the most popular baked good in Japan is *anpan*, soft rolls generously filled with sweet red bean paste. It is so beloved that there is even a children's cartoon superhero whose head is an anpan, named – you guessed it – Anpanman. Like a lot of Japanese characters, Anpanman's mythos is pretty weird. His defining feature – his soft red bean bun head – is also his weakness, and if it gets wet, damaged or partially eaten (often in an act of self-sacrifice), Anpanman effectively dies until his creator, Uncle Jam, bakes him a new head to replace the old one. But as odd as this backstory is, it's downright upbeat compared to that of Kogepan ('burnt bread'), a San-X character who is also an anpan, but one who falls off the baking tray and into the back of the oven, where he is forgotten and proceeds to burn. Unsellable and unloved, Kogepan spends his days caning milk as if it were beer, wallowing in a jealous funk as his beautifully baked siblings are sold to happy customers.

So yeah. Anpan. Crazy stuff. Don't burn it!

To make the sweet bean paste (known as *anko*), combine the drained adzuki beans in a saucepan with the sugar and bring to the boil over a medium-high heat. Continue to boil, stirring frequently until the liquid reduces to a very thick syrup – you are effectively making a bean jam, so if you have a thermometer, use it; the mixture is done when it reaches 103–105°C (221°F). When the beans are finished, stir in the honey. You can keep the beans whole (called *tsubuan*) or blend to a smooth paste with a stick blender or food processor (*koshian*). Transfer to the refrigerator, uncovered, to chill completely before proceeding.

Use spoons or your hands to form the chilled anko into balls – they should each be about the size of a golf ball, about 40–45 g (1½–1¾ oz) each. After the first rise of the dough, divide it into 12 equal (50 g/2 oz) balls on a lightly floured surface. Using your hands, flatten each dough ball out into a circle about 8–9 cm (3½ in) in diameter; try to make the outer edges of the circle thinner than the centre. Cup each dough circle in your hand, place an anko ball in the middle, then draw up the dough edges and pinch them shut, completely enclosing the an into a bun. Place the buns, seam-side down, on baking parchment-lined baking sheets about 5 cm (2 in) apart, and leave to prove again for about 30 minutes.

Preheat a fan oven to 200°C (400°F/gas 6). Brush the buns with the beaten egg and garnish each one with a little pile of poppy seeds in the middle. Bake for 10 minutes. Leave to cool before eating, but a still-warm anpan is a rare treat, so don't let them cool too long! These last a day at room temperature, or they can be frozen for up to one month; defrost them at room temperature.

GOOEY EGG CURRY BREAD

HANJUKU TAMAGO IRI YAKI KARĒPAN 半熟卵入り焼きカレーパン

MAKES 8 BUNS

40 g (1½ oz) Japanese curry roux
200 ml (7 fl oz/scant 1 cup) water
1 batch of Basic Japanese Bread Roll
    Dough, page 185
plain (all-purpose) flour, for dusting
8 eggs, soft-boiled and peeled (for timings,
    see Marinated Eggs, page 101)
1 egg, beaten well with a splash of milk
10–15 g (½ oz) panko

For almost as long as they have been eating curry and bread in Japan, they have been eating bread filled with curry. Curry bread, or *karē pan* in Japanese, was invented in or around the 1920s, and remains a firm favourite, sold not only at bakeries and convenience stores but also dedicated curry restaurants, who often offer house-made curry pan as a takeaway item, sort of like a souvenir. Typically, curry pan is deep-fried, like a doughnut. But it works very well baked, too, which is what this recipe is for.

Reconstitute the curry with the water. You can either do this in a saucepan or the microwave – for the latter, simply heat the roux and the water together in 30-second bursts, stirring in between each cook until completely dissolved and thickened – this should take about 2–3 minutes in total. Leave the curry in the refrigerator to cool completely while you prepare the rest of the recipe.

After the first rise of the dough, divide it into 8 equal (75 g/2½ oz) balls on a lightly floured surface. With a rolling pin, flatten each ball out into a circle about 15 cm (6 in) in diameter; make the outer edges of the circle thinner than the centre. If the centre of the dough is stretched too thin, the buns could rupture while baking. Place a big spoonful of the chilled curry sauce in the middle of each dough circle, and place an egg on top of the curry. Draw up two dough edges on either side of the buns and pinch them together at the top of the egg. Draw up the other two edges, pinching them together on top of the other dough seam to completely enclose the egg and curry. Place the sealed buns, seam-side down, on baking parchment-lined baking sheets about 5 cm (2 in) apart, and leave to prove again for about 15 minutes.

Preheat a fan oven to 200°C (400°F/gas 6). Brush the rolls with the beaten egg and sprinkle each one with a large pinch of panko. Bake for 15 minutes, and leave to cool slightly before eating. You can also serve these at room temperature and they will last for a day in the refrigerator.

HOT DOG ROLL
SŌSĒJI PAN ソーセージパン

MAKES 8 BUNS

1 batch of Basic Japanese Bread Roll
  Dough, page 185
plain (all-purpose) flour, for dusting
8 small (about 70–80 g/2½–3 oz each)
  cooked, hot dogs – I use Helen
  Browning's and they are perfect,
  or you can use Japanese sausages,
  such as NH brand
1 egg, beaten well with a splash of milk
about 25 g (just under 1 oz) each ketchup,
  mayonnaise and tonkatsu sauce
flat-leaf parsley leaves and/or chives,
  finely chopped, to garnish
a few pinches of poppy seeds
  and/or sesame seeds
pepper, as needed

I wasn't sure what to call this recipe. In Japan it's *sōsēji pan*, which just means 'sausage bread,' and is technically correct, but it sounds weird. Then I thought about 'hot dog bun', but that's misleading, because of course a hot dog bun is just a bun, not a bun with a hot dog already inside it. How about sausage roll? Again, that's something else. So, I settled on 'hot dog roll', because that feels pretty accurate – this is essentially a hot dog-esque sausage, baked directly into a bread roll, with various condiments.

After the first rise of the dough, divide it into 8 equal (75 g/2½ oz) balls on a lightly floured surface. Form the balls into oblongs, slightly shorter in length than the sausages themselves. Press a sausage into the centre of each oblong, and draw up two flaps of dough from the sides, pinching them together in the middle of the sausage. Ensure the dough is strongly sealed around the hot dog, or the rolls may split during baking. Transfer to the baking parchment-lined baking sheets, at least 5 cm (2 in) apart. Preheat a fan oven to 220°C (425°F/gas 7). Brush the dough and sausage with the beaten egg, then squeeze the ketchup, mayonnaise and tonkatsu sauce over the top of the sausage. Scatter the parsley and/or chives, poppy seeds and sesame all over. Bake for 12 minutes and leave to cool slightly before eating. These last for a day in the refrigerator and reheat well in a hot oven.

EGG SANDWICH, THREE WAYS

TAMAGO SANDOICCHI SAN-SHU 卵サンドイッチ3種

MAKES 2 SANDO

Like a lot of things in Japan, there is an enormous amount of variation on the humble egg sandwich. At its most basic, it is pretty much indistinguishable from an ordinary egg mayo sandwich, except by the use of Japanese mayonnaise. But these are often embellished and remixed, usually with more eggs, in different forms. For example, you can get egg sandwiches with runny or fudgy boiled eggs in them, or Japanese-style omelettes. It's not common to find all three together, but I figured ... why not!? I'm American. And in America, too much is never enough.

The method here, by the way, is adapted from one Tim Hayward posted on Instagram that he came across while researching his excellent book of bread and sandwiches, *Loaf Story*. It's based on scrambled eggs, which makes a very creamy, fluffy egg mayo with a delicate, irregular texture. However, if you'd like to use hard-boiled eggs, that's fine, too.

Melt about one third of the butter in a small frying pan (skillet) set over a medium-low heat. Season the eggs well with salt, MSG and pepper, then pour them into the pan. Scramble them with a whisk for about 3 minutes until almost completely set, then remove from the heat, whisk in the remaining butter, then tip everything into a cold bowl to stop the cooking. Leave to cool for about 5 minutes, then beat in the mayonnaise with a spatula and transfer the egg mayo to the refrigerator to chill completely. Taste and adjust the seasoning as needed.

Spread the egg mayo onto the bread, making a slight mound towards the middle. Scatter some sea salt on top and cover with the other slice of bread. Slice in half and enjoy, or wrap in cling film (plastic wrap) and keep in the refrigerator for up to two days if made with shokupan; if made with supermarket white bread, it will only keep for a few hours.

15 g (½ oz) butter
4 eggs, very lightly beaten (just break the yolks and stir them up a bit)
salt, MSG and pepper, to taste
4 tablespoons mayonnaise, ideally Japanese Mayo (page 207), cold (straight from the refrigerator)
sea salt
4 slices of bread, ideally shokupan (pages 183–184)

THE DOUBLE EGG SANDO

Follow the instructions on page 193, but
add 3 medium-boiled eggs (cooked for about
6½ minutes from room temperature, or 7 minutes
from the refrigerator). Peel the eggs, cut them in
half and line up three halves over the middle of
each sandwich, on top of the egg mayo, so that
when you cut the sandwiches you will expose
the orange yolk. Season the eggs with a little
extra sea salt.

THE TRIPLE EGG SANDO

Follow the instructions for the double egg sando
left, but add a half quantity of dashimaki tamago
(page 97). (Make the full recipe and then just use
half, rather than making half the recipe.) Slice the
omelette and lay it in between the egg mayo and
the boiled eggs.

THE TONKATSU SANDWICH

ZA TONKATSU SANDOICCHI ザ・豚カツサンドイッチ

MAKES 2 KATSU SANDO

300–350 g (10½–12 oz) pork fillet,
    pork loin (rind removed), or minced
    (ground) pork
salt, pepper and MSG, as needed
1 egg
1 tablespoon water
1 teaspoon oil
30–40 g (1–1½ oz/¼–⅓ cup) plain
    (all-purpose) flour
40–50 g (1½–2 oz/⅔–scant 1 cup) panko
oil, for deep-frying
4 slices of good-quality sandwich bread,
    ideally shokupan (pages 183–184)
about 10 g (½ oz) butter
60 g (2 oz) mayonnaise
2 big handfuls (a bit less than a quarter)
    of sweetheart (hispi) cabbage,
    very finely shredded
30–40 g (1–1½ oz) tonkatsu sauce

Tonkatsu sandwiches (a.k.a. katsu sando) ought to be kept simple. But that doesn't mean they don't warrant thoughtful consideration. First and foremost, a katsu sando should be easy to bite through, which means no tough bread, and no chewy pork. Secondly, it should be relatively straightforward to prepare and cook, because katsu sando should be there when you need them, just like they are in conbini. Which brings us to a third criterion: katsu sando should still be good after a day or two in the refrigerator. Finally, keep it simple with the accoutrements: tonkatsu sauce is a must, plus shredded cabbage, and not much else. And that is perhaps the most important criterion of all: a katsu sando should never be challenging in any way. It should be comforting and satisfying, easy to cook and, of course, even easier to eat.

First, make the tonkatsu. If you are using fillet, divide it into two steaks and place them between two sheets of cling film (plastic wrap). Bash the steaks into flat, oblong patties with a rolling pin, with a diameter almost but not quite as wide as the bread you're using (usually about 12 cm/5 in). If you are using minced pork, form it into two firm patties of a similar shape. The loin can be left as is, but you may wish to remove the fatty rib end, depending on your preference for pork fat. Season the pork well on both sides with salt, MSG and a little pepper.

Beat the egg together with the water and the 1 teaspoon of oil. Dredge the pork in the flour, then the beaten egg, making sure to let the pork sit in the egg for a minute so the flour can fully absorb it and form a kind of glue, and then finally pack the panko into the surface of the pork well to ensure an even coating. Pour a 1 cm depth of oil into a deep, wide saucepan, and heat to 180°C (350°F) (use a probe thermometer for this). Fry the pork for about 4 minutes on each side until nicely browned. Drain on paper towels and leave to rest while you prepare the rest of the sandwich.

Lay the bread out on the counter and butter one side of it, and spread the mayonnaise on the other side. Place a nice big mound of cabbage on top of the mayonnaise, then drizzle over a good amount of the tonkatsu sauce. Place the pork on top of the cabbage, then add another little drizzle of sauce. Place the buttered bread on top of the pork, and cut off the crusts, if you like. Cut the sando in half and eat straight away, or wrap them well in cling film (plastic wrap) and keep in the refrigerator, where they'll be good for about two days if made with shokupan; if made with supermarket white bread, it will only keep for a few hours.

POTATO SALAD SANDWICH

POTETO SARADA SANDO ポテトサラダサンド

MAKES **2** SANDWICHES

200 g (7 oz) floury potatoes
5 cm (2 in) chunk of cucumber, halved
    and seeds removed
¼ carrot, peeled
salt, as needed
40 g (1½ oz) mayonnaise
½ teaspoon Dijon or wholegrain mustard
MSG and pepper, to taste
1–2 tablespoons chopped pickles –
    these can be gherkins (cornichons),
    or something Japanese such as smoky
    pickled daikon (page 63)
about 10 g (½ oz) butter, at room temperature
4 slices of white bread, ideally shokupan
    (pages 183–184)
2–4 slices of ham

Carb-on-carb sandwiches are underrated. Caterer extraordinaire and Instagram sensation Milli Taylor made one once that was rendang-flavoured instant noodles, slicked with butter and stuffed between two slices of white bread. I recreated it at home and, my god, was it good. Thatsandwich is similar to one of Japan's most popular sandwiches, yakisoba pan, which are stir-fried noodles in a hot dog bun. But I also enjoy another carb-on-carb conbini staple, the potato salad sandwich – which is exactly what it sounds like. The cool, creamy potatoes are simply sublime on top of squishy Japanese bread – a rhapsody in off-white, a perfect, pillowy carb cloud.

Peel the potatoes and cut them into big chunks, about 2.5 cm (1 in) thick. Place in a saucepan, cover with water and bring to the boil, then cook for about 10–12 minutes until soft. Drain well and leave to dry out and cool completely. Meanwhile, slice the cucumber and carrot as thinly as you can, then sprinkle them with a good amount of salt and let them sit for about 20 minutes to tenderise. Then rinse them under cold running water to remove the salt and squeeze out any excess liquid. Stir together the mayonnaise, mustard and a big pinch each of salt, MSG and pepper. With a fork or sturdy whisk, roughly smash the mayonnaise mixture into the cooked and cooled potatoes, so the potatoes are half-mashed and become one with the mayonnaise. Mix in the cucumbers, carrots and pickles, then taste and adjust the seasoning to your liking.

    To assemble the sandwiches, spread a thin layer of butter on each slice of bread and lay the ham slices onto two of them. Pile the potato salad onto the ham and top with the remaining slices of bread. Slice them in half to serve; if you're having them later, wrap them tightly in cling film (plastic wrap) and keep them in the refrigerator for up to two days.

BLUEBERRY CHEESECAKE
SWIRL SANDWICH

BURŪBERI SANDO ブルーベリーサンド

MAKES 2 SANDO – ENOUGH FOR 4 PORTIONS

1½ tablespoons double (heavy) cream
3 tablespoons icing (confectioner's) sugar
150 g (5 oz) cream cheese
½ teaspoon vanilla extract or paste
2 tablespoons blueberry jam
2 handfuls (about 60 g/2 oz) of blueberries
4 slices of white bread, ideally shokupan
    (pages 183–184), crusts removed

Enabled by Japanese bread's soft crumb and mellow sweetness, the fruit sandwich has been a staple of Japanese convenience stores, bakeries and coffee shops for ages. A recent innovation sees the typical cream replaced with sweetened cream cheese, to make what is essentially a cheesecake, in sandwich form.

Whisk together the double cream and icing sugar until the sugar dissolves, then whisk in the cream cheese and vanilla and beat well until thick and smooth. Fold in the blueberry jam to make lovely swirls. Divide the cream cheese mixture equally onto each slice of bread, then scatter the blueberries over two of the slices. Top with the remaining slices so that the blueberries are in the middle. To serve, cut into triangles and enjoy with a nice cup of coffee. These last for up to two days in the refrigerator.

MELON CUSTARD-FILLED MELONPAN

MERON KURĪMU IRI MERON PAN メロンクリーム入りメロンパン

MAKES 8 BUNS

**For the Cookie Dough
(make this first)**

100 g (3½ oz/1 cup) salted butter,
    at room temperature
70 g (2½ oz) golden caster (superfine)
    sugar, plus more to garnish
30 g (1 oz) light brown sugar
1 egg, at room temperature
1 teaspoon vanilla extract
½ teaspoon melon essence
240 g (8½ oz/1⅞ cups) plain
    (all-purpose) flour
½ teaspoon baking powder

Melonpan – essentially a sweetened bread roll with a crunchy cookie topping, vaguely resembling a melon – is one of Japan's most iconic bakes. But to be honest, I was never that into them. They're a bit plain, a bit dry, a bit *meh* for me. That is, except the kinds that are filled with custard or cream, which I absolutely love. My favourite melonpan in Japan came from a chain bakery called Yamazaki, which made this psychedelically artificial melonpan with a green cookie top and a fluorescent orange-coloured, melon-flavoured custard middle. It was basically like a custard doughnut but with the intoxicating aroma of melon.

This recipe is a bit of a project and you will need a stand mixer, but I promise you it is worth the effort – the end result is a symphony of melon and a wonderful combination of doughy, creamy and cookie-crunchy textures. It's based on a recipe by Shihoko Ura of the blog *Chopstick Chronicles*, and I encourage you to check out her version for some lovely photos of the process.

In a stand mixer with the paddle attachment, beat the butter and sugars until pale and fluffy. Scrape down the sides once or twice during this process to ensure the ingredients are well mixed. Add the egg, vanilla extract and melon essence and continue to beat until incorporated. Finally, add the flour and baking powder and mix until it forms a dry, solid dough. Pack this into an even layer in a rectangular container, cover and refrigerate for at least an hour.

MELON PAN FILLING

Combine the cantaloupe with the cream and sugar in a saucepan and bring to a simmer, stirring occasionally to ensure the sugar dissolves. In a bowl, whisk together the egg yolks, flours and half the milk to form a smooth paste, then whisk a little of the cantaloupe cream into the yolk mixture to temper. Add all of the tempered yolk mixture to the pan along with the salt and milk powder and simmer for about 5 minutes, stirring constantly with a spatula. Whisk in the remaining milk, melon essence, vanilla extract and food colouring and simmer for another 2 minutes, continuing to stir. Purée everything with a blender, then pass through a sieve into a container. Cut a piece of baking parchment and press it directly onto the surface of the custard to prevent a skin from forming, then transfer to the refrigerator and leave to cool completely (about an hour).

BREAD

Follow the instructions for the dough, but add the food colouring at the beginning of the mixing process. Don't add too much – you want a nice, light honeydew colour, not a really bright green. Once the dough has been kneaded, divide it into eight pieces, and roll each one into a little ball. Place the balls on baking parchment-lined baking sheets, at least 5 cm (2 in) apart, and leave to prove for another 30 minutes or so.

TO ASSEMBLE, BAKE AND FINISH

Preheat a fan oven to 180°C (350°F/gas 4). Cut the cookie dough into eight equal pieces, and roll each piece into a ball. Roll each cookie dough ball out into rounds about 11 cm (4⅓ in) in diameter and about 5 mm (¼ in) thick, then drape these over each bread dough ball, gently patting them all around to stick them to the bread dough without knocking the air out. Score the cookie dough very lightly in a diamond pattern and sprinkle liberally with golden caster sugar. Bake for 15 minutes, then remove and leave to cool completely.

Transfer the melon custard to a piping bag fitted with a metal nozzle. If the custard is very stiff, stir it well and it will soften. Use a chopstick to poke a hole deep into one side of each bun and jostle the chopstick around inside to carve out a cavity. Fill each bun generously with the custard. These will keep for a couple of days in an airtight container at room temperature, and I think they are actually better on the second day.

For the Melon Custard Filling (make this next)

100 g (3½ oz) very ripe cantaloupe, diced
200 ml (7 fl oz/scant 1 cup) double (heavy) cream
100 g (3½ oz/scant ½ cup) golden caster (superfine) sugar
3 egg yolks
15 g (½ oz) cornflour (cornstarch)
5 g (¼ oz) plain (all-purpose) flour
5 tablespoons whole milk
pinch of salt
10 g (½ oz) milk powder
1 teaspoon melon essence
1 teaspoon vanilla extract
orange food colouring, as needed

For the Bread

1 batch of Basic Japanese Bread Roll Dough (page 185)
green food colouring or matcha powder (optional)

FUNDAMENTALS

DASHI 出汁

I almost didn't include a recipe for dashi, because there's really no need for it – this book is all about convenience, so you should really be using dashi powder or concentrate. But it feels sacrilegious somehow to not include a recipe for dashi from scratch, because it is so fundamental to Japanese cuisine. If you make this, use it in something where you can really taste it, such as classic takikomi gohan or nanban soba.

MAKES ABOUT **500** ML **(17** FL OZ/**2** CUPS**)**

10 g (½ oz) kombu (about a 10 × 10 cm/4 × 4 in piece)
2 dried shiitake mushrooms
600 ml (20 fl oz/2½ cups) water (for really good dashi, use soft water – it will provide a fuller flavour)
15 g (½ oz) katsuobushi

Place the kombu and mushrooms in a saucepan and pour in the water. Place the pan on a low flame and very slowly bring it to the lowest of simmers; when just a few small bubbles break the surface of the water, add the katsuobushi, remove from heat, and leave to infuse for an hour to maximise flavour. Pass through a fine sieve and gently squeeze out the ingredients. If you're not using it straight away, keep in the refrigerator – it will last about a week, but is better within a few days.

TSUYU つゆ

Tsuyu is a fortified, seasoned dashi, which can be used as a condiment or diluted to make broth for soup. Store-bought tsuyu is yummy and inexpensive, so if you're going to bother making it from scratch, you should make it from real kombu and katsuobushi, which gives it a very full, rich flavour.

MAKES ABOUT **225** ML **(8** FL OZ/SCANT **1** CUP**)**

100 ml (3½ fl oz/scant ½ cup) soy sauce
100 ml (3½ fl oz/scant ½ cup) mirin
60 ml (2 fl oz/¼ cup) sake
50 ml (1¾ fl oz/3 tablespoons) water
1 tablespoon brown sugar
10 g (½ oz) kombu
10 g (½ oz) katsuobushi

Combine all the ingredients except the katsuobushi in a saucepan and leave to infuse for 1 hour. Place the pan over a medium heat and bring the liquid to a low simmer, then remove the kombu and add the katsuobushi. Let the liquid boil, then remove from the heat and leave to infuse for 10 minutes. Pass the tsuyu through a sieve, gently squeezing the liquid out from the katsuobushi. Keep in the refrigerator and use within a month. To use as a broth for soup, dilute 75 ml (5 tablespoons) tsuyu with 275 ml (9⅓ fl oz/just over 1 cup) water to yield 350 ml (12¼ fl oz/1½ cups) – the right amount for a bowl of noodles.

MASTER PONZU　　　　熟成ポン酢

Ponzu is perhaps the only Japanese condiment you definitely should make from scratch. There are some good ones out there, but the best ponzu really captures the 'whole fruit' sensation of fresh citrus, which is very difficult for pasteurised, shelf-stable products to accomplish. Also, if you make your own, you can blend citrus and adjust it to your taste. I make my ponzu in the winter, when good citrus is in season, then keep it going throughout the year like a master stock – I start with the below recipe and top it up with two parts citrus juice, two parts soy sauce and one part mirin, as needed. This results in an evolving, complex, balanced ponzu with a perpetually fresh citrus flavour.

MAKES ABOUT 225 ML (8 FL OZ/SCANT 1 CUP)

5 tablespoons lemon, lime, bergamot and/or yuzu
    juice; you can also add less sour citrus juices,
    such as satsuma, blood orange or grapefruit,
    but remember that ponzu should be quite acidic
5 tablespoons soy sauce
2 tablespoons water
2 tablespoons caster (superfine) sugar
1 tablespoon mirin
1 teaspoon vinegar
¼ teaspoon dashi powder
¼ teaspoon salt
spoonful of citrus zest, crushed to release their oils

Mix everything well until the sugar dissolves. Keep in a jar in the refrigerator indefinitely; top up with more citrus juice and seasonings as needed to keep a perpetual ponzu.

JAPANESE BROWN SAUCE　　　ソース

This is an all-purpose Japanese brown sauce recipe that will work well in place of tonkatsu sauce, okonomiyaki sauce and other similar condiments.

MAKES ABOUT 300 ML (10 FL OZ/1¼ CUPS)

1 teaspoon tomato purée (paste)
1 teaspoon Marmite
¼ teaspoon mustard (Dijon or English)
1 pinch of garam masala
    or mild curry powder
75 g (2½ oz) brown sugar
5 tablespoons ketchup
5 tablespoons HP or similar
    brown sauce
2 tablespoons tamarind paste
2 tablespoons Worcestershire sauce
1 teaspoon rice or cider vinegar

Stir together the tomato purée, Marmite, mustard, garam masala and brown sugar to make a thick paste. Whisk in the ketchup, brown sauce, tamarind paste, Worcestershire sauce and vinegar, until smooth. This is best made at least an hour before you need it to let the sugar and spices dissolve properly. To make this more suitable for okonomiyaki, add an additional 1 tablespoon brown sugar, 1 tablespoon oyster sauce and a little more garam masala. For yakisoba, add 2 tablespoons tsuyu, reduce the sugar to 50 g (2 oz) and omit the vinegar. Keep in the refrigerator for up to six months, in a squeeze bottle.

JAPANESE MAYO　　　マヨネーズ

Most of the recipes that call for mayonnaise in this book don't require Japanese mayonnaise – but that's a bit like saying that toast doesn't require butter. Use it if you got it!

MAKES ABOUT 225 ML (8 FL OZ/SCANT 1 CUP)

1 teaspoon nutritional yeast flakes
1 tablespoon Dijon mustard
1 teaspoon vinegar
½ teaspoon soy sauce
½ teaspoon MSG
200 g (7 oz) mayonnaise

Stir together the yeast flakes, mustard, vinegar, soy sauce and MSG until the MSG and yeast flakes dissolve. Stir this into the mayonnaise and transfer to a squeeze bottle. Keep in the refrigerator for up a month.

GLOSSARY

ABURAAGE 油揚げ
Sheets of puffed, fried tofu, sold frozen at
Asian grocers

AONORI 青のり
Green seaweed flakes, used as a garnish

BURDOCK (GOBŌ) ごぼう
A long, earthy root vegetable; found at Asian grocers

CHICKEN STOCK POWDER 鶏ガラスープ粉
Asian-style chicken stock powder, found in yellow
tins at Asian grocers

CHILLI OIL ラー油
Chinese, Japanese or similar East Asian crispy
chilli oil (do not use European chilli oil)

CURRY ROUX カレールー
Pre-made Japanese curry blocks that are made
into sauce by stirring through boiling water;
common brands include Golden, Java, House
and Yutaka

DAIKON 大根
A large white radish, also called mooli

DASHI 出汁
Broth made from kombu (dried kelp) and
katsuobushi (dried, smoked tuna) that constitutes
the basic flavour of many Japanese dishes;
it can be made from scratch, but in home cooking
is more commonly made from a powder
or concentrate

GOCHUJANG ゴチュジャン
Korean fermented chilli paste

HIJIKI ひじき
Dried, black seaweed with a nutty flavour

JAPANESE BROWN SAUCE ソース
A classic Japanese fruit-based sauce with many
variations including tonkatsu, okonomiyaki,
takoyaki and yakisoba sauces; in most cases,
any will do, but certain recipes call for certain
variations

KAMABOKO 蒲鉾
Pink and white Asian-style fish cakes, sold frozen
at Asian grocers

KATSUOBUSHI 鰹節
Flakes of smoked, fermented, and thoroughly
dried tuna loin, used for making dashi and
as a garnish

KIMCHI キムチ
Korean-style spicy fermented greens, usually
Chinese leaf

KOMBU 昆布
Dried kelp, used for making dashi and other
seasonings

KONNYAKU 蒟蒻
A near-flavourless, bouncy jelly made from the
starch of the konjac plant, sold in Asian grocers

LOTUS ROOT　　　　　　　レンコン
A large, starchy, tubular vegetable full of holes,
available at Asian grocers

MIRIN　　　　　　　　　味醂
Highly sweetened cooking sake; for a stronger
flavour, buy hon-mirin (true mirin)

MISO　　　　　　　　　味噌
Seasoning, usually in paste form, made from salted
and fermented soybeans; white miso is younger
and has a lighter flavour, while red is aged longer
and tastes richer

MSG　　　　　　　　　味の素
Sodium salt of the glutamic acid for providing
umami flavour, found in cute little shakers with
a panda face on them, as well as in larger sacks;
sold under the brand name Accent in the US,
and as Ajinomoto elsewhere

NATTŌ　　　　　　　　納豆
Fermented soy beans with a strong taste and
aroma and a sticky texture; a favourite for
breakfast in Japan

NORI　　　　　　　　　海苔
Sheets of dried seaweed, typically used for sushi
or onigiri

PICKLED GINGER　　　がり・紅生姜:
Ginger preserved in a brine of vinegar, salt and
sugar; the pink and thinly sliced variety (*gari*)
is used exclusively as a condiment for sushi; the
red, julienned kind (beni shōga or *kizami shōga*)
is used as a topping

PONZU　　　　　　　　ポン酢
A citrus-based seasoning or dip, typically made
with soy sauce

RAMEN　　　　　　　　ラーメン
Wheat noodles containing alkaline salts to
make them springy, or the noodle soup dish
that contains them

RICE VINEGAR　　　　米酢
Mild vinegar made from fermented rice
or sake lees

SAKE　　　　　　　　日本酒
Japanese national beverage and ingredient made
from the complex fermentation of rice; in cooking,
it is used for balance, aroma and umami

SANSHŌ　　　　　　　山椒:
The Japanese cultivar of Sichuan pepper, with
a refreshing fragrance and delicate tingle

SHICHIMI　　　　　　七味唐辛子
Shorthand for shichimi tōgarashi, a blend of seven
aromatic spices including chilli, orange and sesame

SHIITAKE　　　　　　椎茸
Meaty mushrooms that become stronger
in flavour when dried

SOBA　　　　　　　　そば
Thin buckwheat noodles

SOY SAUCE　　　　　醤油
Seasoning made from fermented soybeans and
wheat; all-purpose soy sauce is called shōyu and
works for most dishes, but you may also wish
to purchase tamari (dark soy sauce) and usukuchi
(light soy sauce); do not use continental Asian soy
sauces in Japanese recipes

TAKIKOMI GOHAN　　炊き込み御飯
Rice cooked together with various ingredients
in the same pot

TOFU　　　　　　　　豆腐
Curd made from soy milk; recipes specify silken
(kinugoshi) or cotton/block (momen) as needed;
note that firmness levels do not indicate the type
of tofu

TSUKUDANI　　　　　佃煮
Sea vegetables or seafood preserved
in a reduction of soy sauce and sugar

TSUYU　　　　　　　つゆ
Highly seasoned dashi used as a dip
or as a concentrate for broth

UDON　　　　　　　　うどん
Very thick, slippery wheat noodles

WAKAME　　　　　　若芽
Leafy, tender, green seaweed sold dehydrated,
commonly found in miso soup

YUZU　　　　　　　　柚子
Japanese hybrid citrus with tart,
highly aromatic juice

RESOURCES

If you would like to learn more about this sort of day-to-day Japanese home cooking and meal prep, there is a wealth of information available both online and in print. As always, I highly recommend Shizuo Tsuji's *Japanese Cooking: A Simple Art* as the definitive text for both beginners and experienced students of Japanese cuisine – if you don't have it yet, buy it now!

For bento in particular, there are several excellent books in English. My favourites are Makiko Itoh's *Just Bento Cookbook* and its sequel; *Effortless Bento,* from the Japanese publishing house Shufu no Tomo; and for something more modern, Sara Kiyo Popowa's *Bento Power*. Other books I love that contain many bento-friendly recipes include Aya Nishimura's *Japanese Food Made Easy* and Maori Murota's *Tokyo Cult Recipes*. For donburi, ramen and similar hearty bowl food, look no further than Tadashi Ono and Harris Salat's *Japanese Soul Cooking* which contains a wide range of classic noodle and rice dishes.

However, for me the greatest resource of both bowl and bento recipes is the internet, specifically online magazines and easy Japanese recipe Instagram accounts, including but not limited to @delishkitchen.tv, @coldmeal.jp, @orangepagecooking, @cookpad_tv, @setuyaku_gohann, @sasayan_kurashi, @kurashiru, @macaroni_news, and @3puncooking_ntv. Yes, these are all in Japanese, but some of them add English translations and some of them feature recipes in the captions of each post, so you can use the translate function in Instagram to get the details. The rest of them are (probably) simple enough for you to get the gist of, even if you don't understand Japanese. They are well worth a follow for inspiration, as are the hashtags #つくりおきおかず (tsukuriokiokazu – prep-ahead sides) and #一汁三菜 (ichijū sansai – one soup, three sides).

I could go on, but the truth is there are too many good sources of Japanese recipes to name. All I ask is that you don't stop here. One cookbook, no matter who writes it (least of all me), cannot do justice to the vastness of Japanese gastronomy. Keep reading, keep learning, and remember, the closer you get to the source, the better. Which is to say: book a flight to Japan as soon as you can!

Holly Arnold: Thank you for everything! Like, literally everything? You have made so many of my dreams come true. You're like an actual fairy godmother.

Kajal Mistry: Thank you for putting this book together so unfathomably quickly, and with such a crack team! Your ability to rally so many talents (and reconcile their schedules) is a testament to your leadership and all-around awesomeness, and it's my pleasure to have made this book with you. I hope we can make many more!

Laura Edwards: Thank you for working your magic once again! Even though this is our third book together, you keep surprising me with how naturally you find beauty in the mundane.

Evi O: What can I say? I am nothing – we are nothing – without you. They say you shouldn't judge a book by its cover; well, all I can say is: fuck that! I'm so grateful that so many people judge my books by your gorgeous covers.

Aya Nishimura: It was a real privilege to work with someone who 'gets it' and was so dedicated to making sure everything looked just right. Thank you for finding so many perfect bowls, bento and more. Please take me on a tour of うどん県 someday!

Esther Clark: Your dedication to sourcing bean sprouts, against all odds, is testament to your dedication in general. You have been such a wonderful person to work with, someone who not only makes food look great, but keeps everything running smoothly. I was particularly blown away by how you were able to make such gorgeous dishes when I was occupied elsewhere!

Jo Cowan: Not gonna lie – on the first day of the shoot, when you were not there, I was super bummed. But the next day you came, and it was like the sun rose on the studio. Thank you for all your help and your limitless positive energy.

MiMi Aye: You are a beacon of correctness – not just editorially, but morally. It's a sincere privilege to have you work on this book, and to call you my friend.

Eila Purvis: Thank you for your incredible professionalism and dedication, not just to this book, but to the past ... five?! It's been so nice to get to know you a bit more throughout this project, especially about your background living in Japan and studying Japanese culture. Let's hope we can both get back there soon!

Ruth Tewkesbury, Laura Eldridge and the Hardie Grant marketing and sales teams: You are the real unsung heroes. None of us would have jobs if it weren't for everything that you do to make these books the successes they are. Thank you so much!

Emiko Pitman: Thank you for continuing to share your knowledge with me, and for checking my Japanese! I couldn't have hoped for a better mother-in-law or おばあちゃん for Tig.

Laura, Tig and Baloo: Thank you for always supporting me and filling my life with love, all in your own ways. I am happiest when I am with you, and I could not write these books without that happiness. (And thanks for being my guinea pigs!)

Felix: Thanks for keeping me motivated, my no longer hypothetical little dude. I'll make you okayu as soon as I can.

ABOUT THE AUTHOR

Tim Anderson is a Wisconsin-born, London-based chef and the author of five previous books on Japanese cookery, listed here from best to worst:

YOUR HOME IZAKAYA
(2021)

NANBAN: JAPANESE SOUL FOOD
(2015)

JAPANEASY
(2017)

TOKYO STORIES
(2019)

VEGAN JAPANEASY
(2020)

Tim has been a student and enthusiast of Japanese food for more than two decades. After studying Japanese food history at university in Los Angeles, he moved to Fukuoka Prefecture to immerse himself in the local food culture. In 2008, he relocated to London, where he turned his lifelong interest in Japanese cooking into a career, following his victory on *MasterChef* in 2011. He ran the ramen house and izakaya Nanban in Brixton and Covent Garden from its inception as a pop-up in 2012 until his departure from the business in 2021. Tim is now training to be a humanist celebrant for nonreligious funerals.

Tim lives in Lee, the Greasy Spoon Capital of London, with his wife Laura, daughter Tig, son Felix and FIV-positive cat Baloo. His favourite Marvel film is *Spider-Man: Into the Spider-Verse*, but his favourite Marvel Cinematic Universe film is *Captain America: Civil War*, and his favourite Marvel comic book series is *The Unbeatable Squirrel Girl*.

INDEX

217

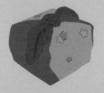

Published in 2022 by Hardie Grant Books,
an imprint of Hardie Grant Publishing

Hardie Grant Books (London)
5th & 6th Floors
52–54 Southwark Street
London SE1 1UN

Hardie Grant Books (Melbourne)
Building 1, 658 Church Street
Richmond, Victoria 3121

hardiegrantbooks.com

British Library Cataloguing-in-Publication Data.
A catalogue record for this book is available from the British Library.

JapanEasy Bowls and Bento
ISBN: 978-1-78488-569-4

10 9 8 7 6 5 4 3

Publishing Director: Kajal Mistry
Acting Publishing Director: Emma Hopkin
Editor: Eila Purvis
Design and Art Direction: Evi O Studio | Evi O.
Illustrations: Evi O Studio | Emi Chiba, Evi O. & Susan Le
Photographer: Laura Edwards
Food stylist: Esther Clark
Prop stylist: Aya Nishimura
Copy-editor: MiMi Aye
Proofreader: Vicky Orchard
Indexer: Cathy Heath
Production Controller: Nikolaus Ginelli

Colour reproduction by p2d
Printed and bound in China by Leo Paper Products Ltd.

花見の桜の木の下で晴れ